THE FREE SPIRIT PONIES PROJECT

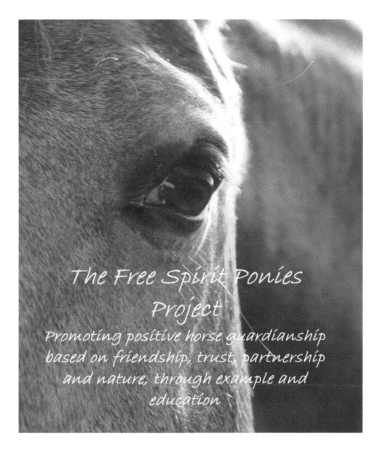

https://www.facebook.com/pages/The-Free-Spirit-Ponies/301243569904837

https://thefreespiritponies.wordpress.com/

For all of the horses and ponies who took the time to
share their lessons and wisdom with me – I am
and always will be eternally grateful.
Thank you.

CONTENTS

8

INTRODUCTION

Anyone who has spent any length of time around horses cannot have failed to have observed some of the profound lessons they are able to teach us. The question however, is whether we have actually learnt from them!

I have been around horses now for over two decades – wow that's scary in itself – and during that time, the horses and ponies I have shared my life with have all had a lesson for me and have taught me some of the most fundamental 'truths' about being a good human and being a compassionate horse guardian.

Inside the covers of this book, you will find some of those lessons that I am now sharing with you so that their legacy can grow and 'ripple' outwards. There have been so many lessons but these are some of what I and the herd consider the most important.

They are presented to you through the pictures I have been lucky enough to take, my thoughts and feelings, including those given to me by our horses and ponies and also through some of the entries I made on our Facebook page and WordPress Blog that illustrate the lesson. They are not in any particular order and can be read as a kind of 'journey' as we have experienced them or as individual gifts of motivation and learning; whichever suits you.

There is a well known saying that "when the student is ready, the teacher will appear" (Buddhist Proverb) - well, my teachers have appeared in the form of horses and continue to do so.

One of the biggest lessons though is that we have control over our lives, much more than we give ourselves credit for. Yes there are things that on the face of it, we cannot do anything about but we can still CHOOSE how we think and feel about them and how we will handle them.

We have choices. We can choose how we react; how we behave and how we treat others around us, including our horses.

It is my hope that the 'lessons' and wisdom contained in these pages and given with love and hope from the horses to each and every one of you, will enable you to choose wisely and from a place of compassion and understanding.

To get us going........

The Life Lessons I have learnt from our horses......

I wrote an entry on our Facebook page on 3rd October 2014 which fits nicely here as a welcome to the observations and reflections in the following pages.......

"When I look back, our herd have taught me so much! More than I could ever have imagined.....so here is a small summary of those 'gifts' ......

MY EQUINE TEACHERS.........

STANLEY gives me confidence when I most need it and is my 'base' my 'soul' , my sanity, my strength, my confidante and my advisor.

WILLOW is my spirit. He reminds me of my purest soul and to be curious and see excitement and joy in everything.

CASPER teaches me to stay 'young at heart' and see the world as a child and that some battles are better avoided and to 'live to fight another day'.

RED is my patience. He reminds me that 'good things come to those who wait' as well as sometimes it's better to remain a step back and observe a situation before 'bowling in'. He is also my reminder of what 'calm leadership' or 'passive leadership' (Mark Rashid) looks like.

TOFFEE is my affection and love. He also shows me how to think 'outside of the box' with his cheeky and clever thinking but also to be ready to protect those we love when needed and in whatever situation.

GIZMO is my courage. He is my 'heart of a lion' and reminds me that even the smallest can be the strongest if we have the belief in ourselves. He is always there to 'prod' me when I need to get on with something or make a decision and just gives me 'that look'

WHIPPER is my independence and reminds me that it's ok to be different and 'quirky' and that it's ok to not 'fit in' all of the time.

SKY is my mirror. She teaches me to confront my fears head on, not to be afraid of being afraid and to be honest with myself about how I'm feeling so that I can move forward. She has also taught me to work from a perspective of health and wellbeing not illness and negativity.

CINDY taught me dignity and wisdom and to have the inner strength and determination to keep fighting until you get what you really need or want

PUZZLE showed me that even the smallest opportunity of happiness, love and life is still a wonderful opportunity and should be grasped with both hands – it is always worth the risk

ANNIE taught me to trust my heart and my instincts even if things seem impossible. She reminded me to see beauty everywhere, even where we least expect it, to see and feel the

11

messages that the universe sends and be grateful for every moment.

FLASH has taught me to really let go of outdated and unhelpful knowledge and beliefs, how to go right back to the beginning, to basics, simplicity, freedom and liberty and meet each other there.

LITTLE SKY shows me how determination and taking chances can pay off and how to be self-reliant and resourceful but above all, to not just survive but to thrive whatever challenges life 'throws' at you.

And of course, WILBER THE PIGGY reminded me that life is an adventure and should be enjoyed, that fresh fruit and veg can be the most exciting things in the world and that there is always time for sleeping deeply and completely, whether that's on the grass in the sun or snuggled up in bed.

Our other pets are also teaching us every day - what have your horses or other pets taught you today?"

Awakenings

"*Have you ever had a moment when something, which you initially think is totally insignificant, happens and that something becomes a defining point for the rest of your life? They talk about don't they, although I've never really worked out who they are. You hear stories about it all the time, about people who change their whole lives in the blink of an eye or people who suddenly see 'the error of their ways' or suddenly snap out the dream-world they've been living in, give up everything they know and do something which seems crazy to everyone around them. I guess maybe I fall into the last category but I'm not sure yet!*

All I know is that one minute I was chatting to a friend at work about how time seems to be flying past and how we were both so tired and stressed all the time. She had bought some books in for me to read because we had talked previously about how the only time I ever relax is when I sit down and get into a good book. Having said that, I don't usually have the time to sit down, let alone read. We've had this conversation before, more than once and I'm sure it's the same conversation millions of other people have every day just before they get back on with filing the paperwork or doing the washing or paying the bills or trying to find a second to call their brother, aunt, dad or closest friend and get a decent night's sleep. It's one of those conversations that get a little deeper into your soul than whether it's going to rain or when your boss wants the latest report by – but not much, not usually by much. It might niggle for a moment and feel a little uncomfortable just for a second, but usually it passes without too much problem and slips back into its cosy little box in the back of your mind somewhere, where you keep the stuff that somehow you know is important but you don't really know why or how – you just have a sneaky suspicion that you probably shouldn't get rid of it altogether. Usually it's a bit like your old bank statements or tax records that you hang onto for several years until you can't fit anymore into your filing cabinet. Finally you have 'a big clear out' and you shred them, somehow knowing that the minute you do, you'll get a letter from the tax office asking for proof of your earnings between 1987 and 2005, the very papers you have just turned into confetti! That's what usually happens with a conversation like that anyway....

Somehow though this time it wouldn't go away, it hung around and it 'bugged' me, like that little voice in your head that most of us ignore the majority of the time because we'd probably think we'd gone a little crazy if we actually listened to what it said! The fact that it's probably the most sensible and honest part of your being has nothing to do with it – there's shopping to be done, and the garden to water and dogs to feed......you get the picture!

Anyway, when I got home that night (after I'd fed and checked my seven ponies and three pigs, poo-picked the field and topped up the water troughs), I decided (after I'd made the tea and loaded the dishwasher, wiped down the kitchen, and got ready for the next day) that I would choose one of the books my friends had given me and at least read a few chapters before I went to bed – if nothing else, maybe it would help me sleep a bit better. So tired but determined and strangely, just a little excited I walked up the stairs to where I had deposited the carrier bag with the stash of new-to-me books.

Oddly as I walked up the stairs I felt a little tingle of a memory from when I was young and friends bringing over blacks sacks full of hand-me-down clothes for us to rummage through. I used to get so excited at the thought of a whole new wardrobe secretly tucked away in the shiny black plastic that sat in the middle of the front room floor, just waiting to be ripped open to reveal the wonderful presents inside. It used to make me smile then and it did the same as I walked up the stairs. I remember feeling quite comforted by that.

Carefully untying the knot in the handles, I took each book out one by one and read the back, you know the bit where it gives you a little summary of the story so you can decide if you want to buy it or not. I made two piles – the ones that I wanted to read first and the ones that I would read after those. It wasn't particularly any kind of calculated decision, more of a gut feeling. When I'd been through all of the books I had my two piles. On my 'read first' pile there were two books and the 'read later' pile had about five. I picked up the two 'read first' books but even before I'd done that, I knew which one I was going to start with – I don't know why, I just did. So, still feeling like I had a couple of tiny butterflies in my stomach, I put the other books back in the bag and went downstairs, made a cup of tea for myself and a coffee for my fiancé and stretched out on the sofa. Funny, just doing that felt good. I opened the cover and started to read.

I always read the acknowledgments and the introductions in a book and the bit where the author explains why they wrote it and how the story came together. It's something I've always done and I suppose it's because I feel like I can get to know the person who 'created' this story and had the courage to write it down. I say courage because I've always wanted to write a book. I have so many stories buzzing around in my head which most of the time get pushed to back with 'the naggingly important conversations'. In fact, I think they're in the box next door to them. I have only recently managed to finish writing any of them down – I don't think I can blame lack of time for that though, it's lack of confidence in the fact that anyone would want to read them anyway. After all, if you write a story down, you're writing it for someone to read, maybe not all of the time sure but most of the time. That takes courage and belief, which is something I've never quite managed to keep hold of when it comes to writing down my stories. We all have stories; very few of us will ever be storytellers. Even as I write this, I have no idea whether my courage will hold or whether it will just become another half started 'I'll finish it one day' story. I guess I'll just have to wait and see.

Going back to the book I had begun to read and reading the authors foreword, I got a very strange feeling. You see, she was talking about how a reader doesn't chose a book, how the book chooses them. It made me hesitate and think back to sitting on the floor with the bag of books and how this one had stuck out from the rest – not in a huge, obvious way but in a quiet, gentle way. I remember thinking what an odd coincidence it was but not much more than that.

I started reading the book and very quickly became lost in a new world. That's why reading helps me to relax because I can escape to someone else's life for a while. I think that why a lot of people read actually. It's funny because when I do read, it makes me wonder why I don't do it more often. I used to all the time a kid. Any place, anytime, I'd be reading anything I could get me hands on. Somehow, on the way through life I've lost that somewhere, along with a lot of other things but that's for later.

The story was of a young teenager who had everything until her dad died and her family had had to move in with relatives. From the first few chapters, I got to know a girl who on the face of it had the perfect life until suddenly it was all ripped out from under her. (The irony was that maybe it wasn't a perfect life after all, but that came later in the book.) The underlying message that was beginning to come out of the story was that she never considered yesterday or tomorrow and lived completely in the moment, which in her case wasn't necessarily a good thing. I remember have a vague sensation as I was reading that I was feeling a little uncomfortable – not physically I mean, it was very comfortable on the sofa... no, I mean emotionally. It was just a passing twinge of something that felt slightly un-nerving. After a moment it was gone so I didn't really think any more about it. I read a bit more and then put the book down to go and have a bath, thinking how 'chilled out' I now felt and that I would hopefully get a good night's sleep as I wouldn't be dwelling on the million and one things that usually seem to pop up in your mind just as you lay down to go to sleep. How wrong was I!

I ran the bath, climbed in and sighed to myself as my body was wrapped in the warm water. I lay there for a moment enjoying the feeling then realising that it was getting late, got down to the business of getting washed, shaving my legs and washing my hair. It wasn't until I got to the conditioner stage that I realised something was very wrong. The relaxed, 'chilled out' feeling I had had a moment before had gone. It had been replaced by something a lot more powerful and it was something I hadn't felt in a long, long time. Actually that's not strictly true, I had felt it very recently. In fact, I had felt it a lot recently. The truth was I hadn't let myself feel it properly. Every time it had been there, I'd pushed it away, far away, further than the other stuff so I didn't have to feel it. I realised I was crying and not just a little bit, I was sobbing. Even then, I remember thinking how odd it was, me with my fingers rummaging through my hair working the conditioner through to the ends as you do but with tears streaming uncontrollably down my face. I realised that I felt deeply and painfully sad and alone. There was a huge sense of loss in my heart that hurt like hell and all I could think about was my mum and how much I missed her and my family and how I hadn't spoken to them for way too long. I cried for them all and I cried for my animals, that I've promised so much to and not yet quite delivered. I cried for all the dreams I had and have which never quite seem to be within my grasp. And right in the middle of all of it, right at the centre, I cried because I couldn't even really remember who I was anymore.

So that was my moment, sitting vulnerable and naked in the bath with conditioner in my hair and tears rolling down my face, all because of a passing conversation and the first few chapters of a book I had been given. What scared me the most though, was that I knew this time it wasn't going to go away and I had no idea what I was going to do about it!"

"Have the courage to follow your heart and intuition. They somehow already know what you truly want to become" *(Steve Jobs)*

That 'moment' happened a few years ago but the feeling I had is still with me. Although you might say it's not horse related so why is it here in this book, for me it was the moment when I had to make a choice about whether I would 'give it a go' or 'accept my lot' and stop wishful-thinking. During the same period I kept getting dreams about my horses in which they would gallop past me down country lanes and I could never quite catch up with them or calm them down. Sometimes I have found that the universe will send us messages and help in whatever way we need to hear or see it and will continue to do so until we acknowledge it and make our choices.

Whatever the reason, it's what has pushed me on to start 'walking the walk' so to speak and to get out there and create the future I want because no one else can do it for me.

That moment became a bit of a catalyst for me as since then I have felt more able to 'see' and be more aware of the lessons and wisdom that is all around me if only I listen. I'm sure it's no coincidence that over the last few years I have been lucky to have connected with so many wonderful people and horses as well as so many other animals and experiences and to have been able to learn and grow because of them.

I am not always the best student and often I need reminders but I will always get there eventually and at least now I'm heading in the right direction!

Moments such as this and those we often experience when with our animals or even when thinking about them can be easily brushed aside because we are too busy or not ready to see or hear them. Next time you get that 'feeling' or you suddenly feel emotional or a sense of dejavu perhaps, stop and see where it takes you. It may not be a smooth trip but it's very likely to worth it in the long run.

"If you want to know where your heart is, look to where your mind goes when it wanders" (Unknown)

A Time To Rest & A Time To Play

If you are anything like me, you'll find it hard to relax and can always find something else that needs to be done or another problem that needs your attention. One of the first lessons (and one that is still on-going) that the herd taught me is that there is a time for everything and everything needs to be in balance for us to be healthy, happy and effective. By pushing ourselves too much or trying to keep going when our bodies or minds are screaming "please take a break" is simply destructive and will lead to us not doing anything very well and likely becoming ill or even risking injury.

It is a lesson that has come very hard to me as for some reason I have become hard-wired to believe that I should be busy and productive. I'm sure this is a result of a lack of confidence in myself and my worth and a reliance on others to assign my value based on how useful or industrious I can be. I also feel that the modern world contributes to this feeling for many people and that there is almost a negative view of wanting to 'take a break' or have some 'time-out'. The crazy thing is that it perpetuates behaviour that is the complete opposite of that which is effective and healthy and makes it harder for us to have time to 'find ourselves' and what makes us happy.

By watching the herd and sharing in the demonstrations they freely display on how to be whole and connected and comfortable with who we are, it is easy to learn that rest is just as important as 'work' or activity and that the world around us has a rhythm or heartbeat that, if we are able to align ourselves with it, will ensure we remain healthy, happy individuals within a universal community.

I was reminded of this lesson on the 12th June 2015….

"I had a lovely evening at the field last night before I went back to work (teaching a human psychology evening class) sitting

with the herd in their field. Our office at work is so stuffy at the moment and I was desperate to be able to 'breathe again'.

It was a hot evening and the herd were in a very restful mood, each standing nose to tail with their partners and friends, gently swishing tails to keep the flies off; heads allowed to droop and a back foot cocked. They were perfectly reflecting how I wanted to feel, after a tiring and airless day in the office - rested, content and relaxed and by sitting with them for an hour or so, I was able to reach a similar state.

As I was sitting watching the bees buzz in and out of the wildflowers, listening to the deep slow breathing of the herd and the earth around me, I noticed that our friends herd in the next field were also resting. It is interesting that our two herds often mirror each other or show concern for each other and I have felt that as far as they are concerned they are part of the same herd or certainly have an affinity and connection with each other. As the sun warmed the ground and the breeze kept the air cool and comfortable, both of the herds and I rested and allowed our bodies to rejuvenate and recharge.

I happened to glance over at one of the surrounding fields and noticed that a horse was being ridden in the distance. This is not an unusual occurrence when you are based in the middle of a very popular horse-keeping area but what struck me about this instance was the horse was being galloped around and around in the fields. I'm guessing they were probably preparing for some kind of event perhaps or 'having a bit of a blast' but the contrast of our two herds of horses and ponies resting and conserving energy in the evening heat and watching the pair galloping around was not lost on me.

One of the biggest gifts we can give our horses is a choice and for us to have an awareness and recognition of their

needs. Understanding that horses, as we and all living beings do, have natural needs and a natural rhythm that allows us all to remain in balance with ourselves, our responsibilities and activities and the world around us has become a central message for me recently – not least because I have been quite clearly made aware of it and the sharing of that message by Gizmo, one of our herd. When we 'go against' that rhythm, initially it might seem that nothing really happens but slowly and surely we feel drained, tired, stressed, frustrated and experience any number of other negative and detrimental effects. The same goes for our horses too. The cumulative effect of ignoring it is ill health, reduced immunity, susceptibility to injury and a feeling of being 'cut off', separate, emotionally charged and at the same time, exhausted.

From this point of view and going back to my evening, it would have been better for the person riding in the field to have 'gone for a blast' on a hack in the woods perhaps, where it's cooler and out of the sun or for the rider to have chosen a different time to ride in the field, if they felt the need to ride. I know there are those who might give all kinds of reasons why I'm being 'judgmental' about what I was seeing and I certainly don't wish to turn this into a debate about riding etc – it just really stuck me that for the horses that were able to choose,

that particular time of day in those conditions was for resting not expending large amounts of energy moving at speed.

By paying attention to, honouring and respecting the choices and needs of our horses we are far more likely to establish a bond of trust, understanding and appreciation that will hugely outweigh anything built without those things. It is that bond that will then 'carry' us both when needed and I do know that to be true as I've experienced it many times. When we meet our horses at least half way and really 'see' them for who they are, I promise they will show you how to create magic and achieve a connection we otherwise can only dream of."

Trust Me I'm A Horse!

"To be trusted is a greater compliment than being loved"
(George MacDonald)

For me this too is one of the greatest lessons our horses can teach us. Trust provides a foundation for everything else, even love. We can trust someone without loving them, perhaps even without liking them initially. Trust is about knowledge and consistency but also about faith (not in the religious sense but in the sense that we have feeling of certainty about a situation or person). It gives us a confidence in something or someone. Horses are very good at being horses given half the chance and we can learn a great deal by simply allowing them to show us how to 'be' with them, how to work and play with them (and other people) and how to negotiate from a position of trust and understanding.

Horses can taught us..........

- To trust ourselves
- To trust the universe
- To trust our instincts and intuition
- To trust our horses
- To trust each other
- To trust

Sadly all too often I see horses and people who are not able to trust, either because that trust has been destroyed by previous experience or because they have never had that faith or belief in anything or anyone. For that reason trust is closely linked with confidence, both in horse and human.

I have lost count of the times that our horses have reminded me to trust my instincts. It is something we do intuitively when we are younger – partly because we haven't been conditioned to act/think/feel certain ways about things but also because it just feels right. As a child, trusting our 'gut' makes sense to us and it should, it's an inbuilt mechanism that we all have – human and animal – and it's designed to keep us safe in its most basic form, although I also am learning it is pretty useful for guiding us to what we most need and what will help us to be happiest.

When we care for horses in our lives, or any animals in our homes, it is all too easy to micro-manage their lives in the mistaken belief that we are protecting them, helping them or even making them happy. Sometimes the very best thing we can do is to trust them to show us what they need or how to help them. I have been guilty many times over the years of basically interfering in one of our herds lives and then wondering why it's not working out as I want it to.

On January 1st 2014 I wrote an entry on our page which showed how Flash trusted us to believe in him and his choices, despite us making it nearly as difficult as we probably could have......

"How far would you go if you thought your decision for your horse was better for them than the one they had made for themselves? I know that's a pretty 'loaded' question as of course, it would depend on the situation and the consequences of the decisions made by both parties.....but if for example, you thought your horse would be far happier with a rug on, bearing in mind it's been raining for days, he lives out in a herd (some of the others now have rugs on) and when you arrived at the field he was shivering and looked thoroughly miserable?

That was the scenario that we had today (in fact it's been 'brewing' for a few days with this crazy wet weather we're having) and on reflection, I am very happy with how we dealt with it and the lessons we have all learnt today.

The weather has been so awful and the field is flooded, albeit not as bad in any way as those poor people in Kent and other areas – we just have knee high mud and surface water everywhere. While we don't normally rug anyone, I keep a 'supply' as at times like this I like to be able to offer each of the boys and girls the choice (we don't have a shelter.....yet.... but they can shelter near the hedges) – most of the time, everyone looks at me carrying a rug and almost says "stop being daft Mum, we're perfectly fine" but the last few days, more and more have chosen to have a little bit of help and I have gladly obliged. Flash however, has continued to decline, even though I have the real sense from him that he would actually like one – he watches each time someone else is rugged and seems to almost say yes and then can't quite bring himself to, when 'push comes to shove'.

Those of you that have been following Flash's story here will know that we (or should I say Darren) has spent the last year developing such an amazing bond with him and showing him that we won't force him to do anything he doesn't want to and he has come so far – bless him.

29

Today, both myself and Darren agreed that we thought he would better with a rug on so that meant we were going to have to 'push' a little.

Darren asked Flash to leave the herd and follow him through the Healing paddock and into a much smaller area of approximately 3 metres by 5 metres which he willing did. Still at liberty although in a confined space so not really 'true liberty', we spent perhaps 30 minutes with him, gently 'asking' him to have his rug on....i.e. me holding the rug and approaching in a passive but positive way, watching every muscle for signs of stress or anxiety and visualising him 'warm and cosy' in his rug, while Darren spoke to him, explaining what we were doing and why, and rewarded him every time he 'stepped out of his comfort zone'.

Over the course of the 30 minutes, Flash felt able to allow me to stroke him while holding the rug and take a carrot by reaching his nose through his headcollar!

Then came the time, as it will in all 'sessions' where you can let human ego and control take you somewhere none of you want to go or you can stop, say thank you and accept the decision your horse is choosing to 'stick with' – when I realised my emotions were seeping through - it was that moment that decided which direction this interaction would take.........and I am proud to say, that despite our worries, anxieties and I will admit, slight frustrations, we thanked Flash for allowing us to have this 'conversation' as despite the fact that we kept asking him if 'he was absolutely sure of his choice', he never once reacted in a negative or defensive way, just kept repeating his answer and by his actions, showing us he understood the questions completely i.e. touching the rug or headcollar and then looking or walking to Darren as if to say ' I do understand, I'd just rather not if that's ok'.

Just to prove that the trust we had built was not damaged he happily walked at liberty, with Darren back the herd and his hay, turning to give Darren a cuddle and a 'kiss' before re-joining his family.

As much as it went against our feelings of what we felt was right for him, after all we didn't get his rug on, I believe we actually achieved so much more today and I for one, am very content with knowing that in 'that moment' – the crucial moment, we declined to use our 'power' over our friend – I know there will be those of you out there thinking 'just do it, it's best for him and he's got to learn who's boss etc' and do you know what.....I could have.......I know all the 'tricks in the book' so it wouldn't have been a problem!! But...we didn't and that was Flash's lesson for us today – I think we passed and have all gained something far more valuable .....the understanding that just because you can, doesn't mean you should..... and that we don't have to always agree, to be able to keep our trust in each other and still be friends – thank you Flash (who by the way, was no longer shivering and was perfectly happily eating the biggest pile of hay when we left, having shoved Stanley off of it!!!)"

Here's an entry from the 28th July 2014 where I had to ask Casper to trust me in the same way.......

"When I got to the field this afternoon, my usual quick head-count and initial check instantly highlighted the fact that we were one bay pony short! Casper appeared to have disappeared!

Well, that was until I wandered down to the end of the field (where the winter paddock will be this year) and there standing by the fence, looking a bit forlorn and agitated was one missing bay pony!!

I looked around the fenceline to see where the 'great escape' had occurred.....nothing, no gaps, no posts loose...nothing - Hmmm so it was either under or over and my guess, being that it's Casper we're talking about, is that it was under - he was very good at the 'grass limbo' when he was a yearling and could almost literally flatten his head, neck and front of his body to stretch under very low electric fencing.

After having a little chat about 'boundaries' - the physical type not behavioural in this case I asked him to follow me to the gate for that paddock. This means moving even further away from the herd, who he had clearly been separated from for quite a while. One of the wonderful things about our girls and boys is that they have learnt that we can be trusted to get them safely back with their friends, even if initially that means taking them even further away (Sky learnt this early on and it's really helped her). I simply assured him that I'd show him the way and if he would kindly follow me, we'd get back to the herd together.

Casper looked at me, looked at the herd, whinnied to them, especially Little Sky who had been quite keen to alert me to his separation when I arrived (they really do love each other even if they do act like an 'ole married couple' most of the time) and then he tucked his head into the gap between my back and my arm and together we walked to the gate, opened it, walked out, closed the gate and took a stroll right around the edge of the field to get back to the part of the field where his friends were. At one point, I laughingly asked if he would mind leaving a bit more of a gap between us as I only had my canvas shoes on and I was a bit worried about him treading on the back of my feet (Ouch) and bless his heart, he slowed for a step or two and increased the distance, still 'in connection' with me but more via energy, rather than physically so I had space to walk....

Even when we reached the herd, he didn't charge off or barge me out of the way.....I asked him to come and get a drink first as I was worried he might be a bit dehydrated with the sun and worrying about being alone. He nudged my shoulder and we walked to water troughs, where he had a long drink, dribbled some into my hand as a 'thank you' and then quietly and calmly wandered over to the herd, straight up to Little Sky who wrapped her neck around him and they stood for several minutes mutually grooming each other (I'm sure she'll nag him later!!)........

All achieved without a headcollar, leadrope or even a treat in sight

I truly love our 'Free Spirit family'.......it is such a privilege to be part of their lives and have them as part of ours.......and to able to simply have a conversation in order to achieve something together, rather than force or 'just do something' without asking first, is exactly the kind of relationship I chose to have with each and every one......... "

Sharing The Message So It Can 'Hold Space'

I'm not sure where I first heard the expression 'holding space' but it really resonates with me for so many reasons. All to often we find ourselves in a position where we believe we are helping, supporting, advising or 'counseling' another person or the horses and other animals who touch our lives, only to find that that support or help is being refused, ignored, pushed away or just simply isn't helping. I have come to learn through our herd that actually that's because it is not our help or support that is needed; that we can't always fix it for another; that's not our purpose or choice to make.

Here is where the concept of 'holding space' comes in. Holding space means being there for someone without judgement, without trying to fix their problems or having an influence on any outcome of THEIR journey. It's not as easy as it sounds as we are almost hard-wired to get involved and fix things. However if we can get it right, it can be the greatest gift we can give both to our human and animal family and friends. It is also one of the most important gifts you can give yourself in the sense of holding space for you to care for yourself without guilt.

The horse world is a competitive place not just in the literal sense of the word but also because everyone seems to know better, have a better way or is keen to divulge the one piece of advice that will make everything right for you and your horse. There are so many different ways to do things and differing opinions on what's ok and what's not that it can be a daunting place to practice objectivity, awareness and individuality before we even get into trying to genuinely help others 'find their way'

I wrote a blog for our website trying to explain how we are all on our own journeys and should be able to 'hold space' for those we meet without judging their journey and their experiences in favour of our own (I've tweaked it slightly so it makes more sense here).

"It's interesting that a post I recently shared on a social media site about a 'new headcollar' (a tongue in cheek advert that was actually promoting relationship, trust and taking time although the video itself showed some discrepancies) has raised issues that I am really struggling personally with and highlighted some interesting points. Issues that I have actually perhaps been trying to avoid personally as I don't yet know the solution.....

Firstly though, I am genuinely blown away by the wonderful people who are in the groups and forums I facilitate and other groups I am part of and with whom I have been able to connect through media such as Facebook - so many people doing so much good for horses everywhere and I realised and was relieved to find I was not alone and certainly not 'daft' or 'crazy'. Some days I sit here at my desk or in the field with the herd and just grin from ear to ear at the incredible people I have 'met' or connected with in the last few years........more than I could ever have dreamed of.....

....and then I look around at my local area and on other more mainstream groups on social media and elsewhere and realise that there is still so much of the journey to travel.

I always refer to my life with horses as a journey because really in the big scheme of things I was a conventional horse-owner not so very long ago and yet because of the horses in my life, my desire to learn and understand and my growing awareness of my 'gut feelings' and 'yucky radar' (love that expression) in a few short years I have completely changed.

Where once I stabled horses, rode every day, wanted to compete, carried a whip (yes I did) and rode in a bit...even using martingales and other such torture devices and although Stan was barefoot, I didn't flinch at horses with shoes...... now

36

I struggle with about 90% of the things I see both on the internet, TV and in real life and desperately want to scream "Can't you see????" at my PC screen or at passing riders at the field.

I am getting to the point honestly!!

You see, for me....the most important lesson though that I have learnt while being in the 'horse world' is that people will defend themselves if attacked, every time and sometimes aggressively - often where I might have felt my 'advice' or observations would be helpful they are seen as arrogant, unsolicited and unwanted comments.

It has even resulted in my 'treatment and care' of my own horses becoming the subject of personal verbal attacks and questioning. It hurts! We all know it does. We just want to help and it's thrown back at us and then heaped on with mountains of justifications for this and that and "look at your horses.....they need a good groom and a stable" or "how can you keep horses and not do anything with them, that's just cruel!" I am not a strong person really; I'm learning to be because if I don't, I don't want to think about the outcome but it's not a natural state for me. I 'feel' those attacks and it chips away at my confidence and makes me question myself – granted less so as time goes on but if I'm not careful, the doubt creeps in.

It also makes me angry......very angry! I have discovered a very scary side to myself on this journey – believe me there is a 'dark Andree' who could happily draw blood and become a one-woman vigilante when faced with some of the things we all see and while I really don't very much like that Andree, I have had to learn to embrace her as part of who I am too because if I don't, that darkness, anger and for want of a better word, 'hatred' will bubble and fester and start to creep into everything I am trying to achieve and destroy it. As a wise man once said.... "Darkness cannot drive out darkness: only light can do that. Hate cannot drive out hate: only love can do that." (Dr. Martin Luther King, Jr.)

The funny thing is though, when I think about it objectively and from the benefit of my 'reasonable' psychology background, that's exactly how I may have made another person feel when I offered the 'wisdom of my thoughts' and told them all the things they were doing wrong and how I think they should do it....albeit in a lovely nice way of course!

Yet, in order to help horses, we have to work with the people who are around them!

It has been shown to me so many times by our herd that we have choices, we always have choices, even if they aren't the ones we would necessarily wish to have!

We can either ignore everyone else, pretend we know best and that they will never get it so why bother and simply carry on in our own little worlds, carrying a niggling desire to help but believing we can't make a difference – I am way too guilty of feeling like this some days!

We can continue to think we are better, faster, more knowledgeable, kinder, more understanding, more empathetic, wiser, more experienced and all those other wonderful things and tell everyone we meet what they are doing wrong, why they should change and how......and then watch their 'backs go up' and the defenses rise as they pull back and protect their own values and beliefs no matter how outdated and irrational.

Or, we can set an example every day of what's possible. We can share knowledge in a neutral, compassionate way, with understanding and respect. We can appreciate where a person is on their 'journey' and guide them, if they are ready for guidance, to the possible alternatives for themselves. We can discuss alternatives in a balanced, non-judgmental way and give and receive information that is useful to us and the others around us in a way that it can be accepted or rejected without penalty or personal or emotional discomfort.

I heard of a concept called 'holding space' recently whereby someone is there for someone else but in a way that allows that person to remain a whole individual, unique and with their own choices – it struck me that for most of us, this is very similar to what we are trying to do for our horses – hold space for them so that they can 'be' who they are and in doing so, we can 'be' who we are.

Most of us who have reached a certain stage of our journey with our horses, and ourselves, will have perhaps reached the point where we would like to work with, live with and be with our horses in a way that is positive for us both, motivates us both, creates good feelings in each of us, brings out the best in both of us and ultimately preserves, honours and enhances the spirit and individuality of us both. That, for me, is what is most important.....not what 'technique or method we use'. If

we can truly meet our horses on 'these terms' then we are certainly heading in the right direction.

What's interesting though is it seems that the more we are aware of this and strive towards this with our horses, in many cases the more intolerant we become of other humans who, we feel, are not where they should be on their journey because 'surely it's obvious isn't it; how can they not see what's right in front of their eyes when the evidence is there! '

Why is it that we so easily get caught up in 'human stuff and ego'?

Pick a subject....barefoot, bitless, liberty work, environment, feeding....we are all heading in the same direction and yet we niggle with each other over the details – it's exactly why I hesitate far more than I want to about sharing particular things on social media. I want to share a message and I endeavour to find pieces which as far as possible share that message or at least enable people to look in the right direction and yet often, I know 'the details' may get pulled apart and the message itself lost. I don't mean we shouldn't view everything objectively and 'scientifically', I just think sometimes we can get so caught up in analysing something we actually miss the bigger picture and the bigger opportunity to bridge the gap. Why? Because all the while we analyse, those we are trying so hard to reach, look on and say 'well if they can't agree amongst themselves, how on earth can I possibly understand it and maybe I'll just stick with what I know because "I've always done it that way!!!!"

I have seen it so often....good people with extensive knowledge and understanding, arguing and attacking each other, albeit mostly politely (although not always) over what in many cases are simply 'stop-overs' on the never-ending journey to be the very best horse guardians we can be, sometimes even the same stop-over but just in a different place. I've done it and found myself getting quite intense about something and then feeling stressed, angry or frustrated afterwards because that person didn't 'see' or 'get it'. The saddest thing is that all the time we bicker amongst ourselves, not only do we get 'stuck' but we also alienate and worse still completely ignore those who might just be looking in our direction for the answers they are starting to seek.

The truth is all of us need to take a breath somewhere and try something out for size, otherwise how will we ever grow. It doesn't mean we will stay there, it just means right now we are at this point.....tomorrow we may be on a completely different path altogether or we even be 'carving a trail through the undergrowth' to a destination as yet unknown. The amazing thing about that is we are moving forward, no matter how slowly. My journey has taken me through conventional ways in all their intricacies, to 'join up' and 'pressure –release', with a brief 'stopover' at 'doing nothing because I was too confused and anxious to move' to 'clicker training', to 'horse psychology and understanding natural behaviours' to 'the cognitive horse' and the 'spiritual horse' and I think I am now at 'the horse as my teacher and friend ' ....who knows where I'll be tomorrow and what I will know then.

I know for me, when I got stuck or when I knew in my heart something doesn't quite feel right (and believe me that used to be a very familiar feeling not so long ago), if someone had pointed out everything I was doing wrong and then continued by 'telling me' how to do it right, I would have probably nodded in the right places and then ignored them because of how they made me feel, regardless of whether the information they gave was valuable or not. It might have been just the answer I was looking for but it would have been lost because of the negative emotion it was given with.

No matter how much we believe what we are doing is right and 'the best way' , we will not be able to pass that on to those who we should really be seeking out, if we continue to deliver with message with arrogance and an "I am better" attitude (even unintentionally) or in way that creates negative emotions for the person receiving the message. Think about the times it's happened to you – how did you feel? I know none of us want to believe we would do that but think about it honestly and objectively and you may discover the truth of the words. I know I have….and all I did was alienate the listener, make the situation worse for the horse involved at the time and leave myself angry, frustrated and feeling useless.

When we meet our horses, we endeavour to meet them as equals, both having a valid position as a thinking, feeling being and in the spirit of creating harmony, cooperation and strengthening our friendship and relationship. Yet, we don't always afford our fellow humans the same. Obviously I am not talking about those who intentionally abuse, and hurt animals – there is a whole other hell for them. No, I'm talking about everyday people like you and I who are trying to do their best with the knowledge they have, no idea where to look and buried up their eyeballs in "we've always done it that way" and "I've been around horses for years so I'm clearly more expert than you" .

After all, we 'don't know what we don't know'! I didn't until I met an abused mare called Carrie and everything I 'knew' crumbled around me! Even then, it wasn't till Stan found his way to me that I really took the hint!

Maybe….just maybe, if we approached the sharing of what we have come to know and what we have learnt on our journeys, through our horses and experiences, with our fellow horse guardians in the same way as we would with our own horses or a horse who has found their way to us; with compassion, empathy, kindness, promoting the positive, honouring their individuality and at the same time recognising that they may be feeling worried, defensive, scared, confused, fearing change, lacking confidence or simply have no idea that things could be different, then just maybe we can really make a difference. We all have so much to give…..and our horses need us to for their sake…..

Don't get me wrong, I am not saying we shouldn't 'say something' or 'do something' if we can, far from it……I honestly believe we should. I'm saying it's about the way we do it and how the other person receives it as well as how they compare that information with what they see us demonstrating. It seems to me that that these are the elements which might determine whether or not that information is accepted or disregarded.

I am in no way perfect when I see things that upset and anger me every day but I am really trying. I'm trying because Stanley and the Free Spirit herd and all the other horses and ponies out there need me to and have asked me to.

So, pack your bags. We still have a long way to go! The journey is likely to be bumpy and fraught with 'danger' and we might stray off the track once in a while and get a bit lost but it will always be worth it - together we can make it and maybe even show others the way."

What's Love Got To Do With It?

So, in the words of Tina Turner "What's' love got to do with it?" Well pretty much everything actually.....

However, when I refer to love here I am not referring to the often one-sided, unbalanced, unrealistic and romanticised version of love that many of us may well recognise, I am referring to real and unconditional love that accepts, honours and celebrates both ourselves, the earth we live on and the other beings that we share our lives with. I mean REAL love!

I once had the privilege of meeting a pony called Bentley while I was visiting our local horse sanctuary. I have felt love, deep love from many horses and ponies, especially our own but this little guy.....his purpose and gift to the world was simply to 'share love'. I don't often get such clear messages as he gave me; usually they are more feelings and a sense of knowing but

Bentley, the beautiful, gentle and infinitely kind Bentley made himself completely clear to me and in doing so, found a special little spot all of his own in my heart. He went on to find a wonderful home and I am forever honoured that I had the chance to meet him and learn from him.

If we had had room I would have offered him a home instantly but that wasn't his destiny or mine – he had a message to spread and he needed to be out in the world doing it. I hope one day our paths cross again as I'd like to let him know how much he impacted on me. Of course, I'm sure he already knew but it would be wonderful to have another Bentley cuddle!

"Real love begins when nothing is expected in return"
(Thích Nhất Hạnh)

Horses have got this love thing completely sorted. If we just watched and followed their examples, we wouldn't end up in half the tricky situations we do. Real love doesn't care what you look like or how 'pretty' you are; it doesn't care if you have the latest gadget or the biggest house - it is nurturing, compassionate and unconditional.

It means we are all part of one big family and the friendships that that family brings. Family as many of us will already appreciate doesn't have to be related by blood although of course, often can be. For me though, family are those closest to you, whether human, horse, dog, cat...whoever.

In this definition of family and of love, it is where we find peace; where we can rest if we need to; where we can be completely free to be ourselves and where we will be accepted and welcomed as such.

On the 24th August 2014, a stallion called Outrageous proved that to me......

"I have spent the most amazing day just 'being' with a herd...or rather a family group....of Highlands belonging to some very dear friends of ours.

It is a true privilege to interact and share space with such a wonderful family and to see and experience first-hand, how allowing an incredible stallion to live the life he needs with a herd of stunningly beautiful mares and their 'children' (who are allowed to grow up naturally in the family unit) creates such harmony, gentleness and love.

When I walked into the field, I simply went and sat on the water trough so as not to disturb the group who were resting under the trees. However they saw me and ventured over to say hello.

Outrageous the stallion waited and then slowly and calmly walked towards me after his 'ladies and children' had said hi. He very gently and precisely moved forward towards me until he was standing with his chest against mine, my head tucked into his neck and his head tucked around my head and resting on my shoulder and there we stood together in silence for possibly half an hour (I don't honestly know as I was 'lost' in his quiet strength and magnificent gentleness) - we breathed together and honestly couldn't have got closer than we did and for the whole time I felt so peaceful and safe, wrapped in the protection of Outrageous

I don't know how he knew that that would be what I would need (I didn't till it happened!) but he did and for those precious moments I felt part of his beautiful family - a feeling that I truly can't find the words for.....

I know that it is not viable or practical or for that matter even remotely sensible, for all male horses to remain stallions and certainly not breeding stallions - there are already too many unwanted and abandoned babies out there - but for those horses whose destiny it is to bring new life into the world, this is the life and the world and the way I truly believe it should be done - Outrageous and his family are living proof of it.........thank you Outrageous for sharing your family, your love and your gift with today, I will treasure it forever"

Our herd has also taught me time and time again that compassion is universal – every living being has the ability to be compassionate as this example from 18ᵗʰ October 2013 with our wonderful Gizmo shows....

"Sometimes the universe comes together to help a situation and although that situation may not work out the way you would like it to...it does work out in the way that it should......

Tonight while we were at the field, Gizmo came away from the herd and 'called' Darren over - Darren thought initially he just wanted a cuddle but Gizmo actually wanted to show him where a very sick little rabbit was hiding in the long grass. We carefully and gently caught the rabbit and placed it in a box filled with straw and hay (thank you for Wilber for letting me raid your bed) and it settled down and tucked itself into the straw. Our landlady fortunately knew someone who does wildlife rescue in Bexhill and she kindly called him for us, only to find he was 5 minutes away doing another job. Within 15minutes he had arrived and was sadly able to confirm that the poor little soul was suffering terribly from mexamatosis (not sure if that's how you spell it) and it would only get worse.

So he quietly and gently took the little rabbit to the vet so that they could help him or her cross peacefully to the Rainbow Bridge without suffering any longer.

Run wild and free little one, the universe came together to find you peace and help you be pain free again and although we hoped you could be saved, perhaps you have been, in the way that was right. Enjoy the endless fields of green and play with your forever family - you shared our lives for a short but sweet time. Thank you Gizmo for your help in freeing a pure soul from pain xxx"

Love is the strongest force in the universe when it is pure and without judgement.

Lessons From Rhum

Sometimes we are privileged to meet a very special soul who may have a special message for us or a particular gift to give - Rhum or Mecredsburn Rhum to give him his proper name was one such teacher.

He was born into a family of Highland Ponies under the care of very dear friends of ours and for a number of reasons was a miracle and a very special gift himself but what he taught us in his short time here has enabled us to help so many more horses and ponies and will continue to do so.

Here's a bit of his story...the part we have the honour of sharing with him.....starting in January 18th 2014.

"We had a wonderful experience today and one that we couldn't have had without the help and wisdom of our herd. A good friend had asked us if we could help with a problem she was having with her 7 month old foal as he had become very nervous and she was worried for him. We spoke via message during the week and I felt it would be far better to go and 'see' what was actually happening so we could make sure any advice we gave was right for this precious baby.

What we experienced was one of the most amazing demonstrations of courage from a gorgeous boy who had found himself in a confusing and un-nerving set of circumstances, through no fault of his or his 'human mums' – it was just a case of bad timing really. He had been weaned quietly and seemingly without problem (He is one of the lucky ones as his family live as a herd in a natural and peaceful environment) and then in all the horrible weather we have had recently, had started to struggle in the cold and wet and needed to come into a stable to dry off and warm up and be checked over for a bit. It appeared to me that this had been a bit of a shock for him and all of a sudden he found himself alone, away from his family and unable to get back to them or use any of his instinctive abilities to react to the situation he was now in. As I say this was no-ones fault and just a set of circumstances which could happen anywhere. What had happened then was that despite being easily approached and handled in the field, he started to get very anxious when people went into his stable and would turn his bottom to them, not to kick or hurt them but basically to try to 'hide in a corner' and stay away. He also became very 'jumpy' with quick movements and people trying to be near him. Our friend became increasingly worried about him – she had bought him in as she needed to for his health and wellbeing and now all she wanted was for him to be able to go back out with his friends and family, but that meant walking a distance, including down a stretch of road so he needed to have a headcollar on and be able to feel calm and trust who was leading him – not a situation that seemed possible.

With our friends help, we spent about half an hour or so with this amazing little man, sitting quietly in his stable, speaking gently to him all the time and telling him how thankful we were every time he tried to come near us and boy did he try......he

*so wanted to….and slowly and quietly he began to trust us
(with the help of a lovely juicy apple which he smelt from a
distance, then licked by stretching his body as far as he could
so he didn't have to come near and then eventually, nibbling a
bit off).*

*Between myself and Darren, using all of the wonderful lessons
our boys and girls had taught us, and the truly enormous
courage and heart of this very special little man, we were
honoured to be part of this heart to heart communication,
which called for complete trust, focus, honesty and ego-less
listening.*

*To watch this beautiful baby tell us what was worrying him and
ask for our help, showing us exactly how we could help him
and allowing us to, even though it was going against what his
instincts were telling him, was one of the most humbling but
incredible experiences I have been part of. By using only
kindness, listening with our hearts not our heads, staying
completely in the moment and generating a positive and
inviting 'bubble', together we turned fear and worry to curiosity
and playfulness, ending with Darren and this very special
young man mutually grooming, while I sat at his feet and
talked to him! The best thing was he chose when to 'end' our
shared time by taking a big deep breathe and turning to eat
his hay, relaxed, calm, and happy while we thanked him for
his trust and for being so honest and quietly left his stable.*

*Later I had a text from my friend to say he had nibbled at her
husband's sleeve when he had gone in to do his evening feed
– a truly enormous and generous step for him and far more
than I would ever have dreamt when we set off this morning.*

*I have posted this not to brag or tell you how wonderful we
are, because we could not have done a thing without the
generosity of this special soul and his loving Mum – I have
posted because what we experienced today was this amazing
baby showing so clearly that if we take the time to meet our*

horses in their worlds, without preconceptions, our horses, no matter how afraid or worried they are, can tell us how to help them and even guide us through the process – we just have to listen with love in our hearts – thank you both for teaching us such an important lesson in such an inspirational way.

This little guy is so special in so many ways, not least of all the fact that he shouldn't even be here at all and yet he is, he has dealt with everything that life has already sent him and with trust and belief, has become a gorgeous playful yearling. I have watched him grow over the last few months and his determination and persistence are incredible.

He may never be the fastest or the most agile but he will always be a fighter and have a heart so big you can feel it 'wrap you up' when you are in his presence (I believe his Dad gave him that ♥)

This little guy is proof that love and belief can 'climb mountains' and he will always have a special place in my heart - just love this little guy to bits"

"Most people do not listen with the intent to understand; they listen with the intent to reply."
(Stephen R. Covey)

Sadly on 13th December 2014, Rhum was called home but he left behind a legacy that we can honour today and always.

"Some of you may remember myself and Darren helping some friends of ours, Dawn and Graham with one of their wonderful Highland babies called Rhum or as he became affectionately known 'Rhum-bum'.

Today, we received the very sad news that little Rhum had passed away and was found this morning by his mum.

Rhum was and always will be an incredibly special young pony – right from the start, because of dedication and love, he beat the odds and despite many unique and individual characteristics, he had a light in him that shone so bright, he touched the hearts and souls of everyone who met him. I think that perhaps when a soul is so pure, they cannot stay for long on earth and are sent to remind us to love deeply and completely, without condition and once that message is given, they need to move on so that we can take the gift they gave us and share it with the world.

I for one, know that he touched our souls when we met him and a piece of our hearts is now journeying with him on the next part of his 'story'......a story that isn't ending but just beginning because he has given us a task to pass the love, determination and complete joy of life that Rhum had and gave to us, to everyone we share our lives with.

We have been privileged and honoured to have been able to share a small piece of Rhum's journey with him – he taught us so much in such a short time and he bought us closer to our friends Dawn and Graham and for that we will always be grateful. His mum Dawn is heartbroken so if you have a quiet moment, please close your eyes and send her love and peace – Rhum, along with his herd mates and family, had a life that many horses can only dream of and no one could have done more to make sure he was happy.

I always dreamt that maybe one day Rhum might be able to join the Free Spirit Herd, after all he always felt like he was a part of our family anyway – now he will able to if he so chooses and I hope he will visit us from time to time as I'm sure he will his mum and dad.

Run wild and free, our special miracle boy – we are eternally thankful for the time we shared. Mecredsburn Rhum 16.6.2013 - 13.12.14."

Holding Sky

Sometimes we can do everything we feel it is in our power to do; we can utilize ever bit of information and knowledge we have and we can use every tool in our toolkit and it still won't be enough.

We learnt that lesson in a very emotional way with firstly Cindy when she had her stroke and lost all mobility and strength in her hind end and then even more so with Puzzle, whose body was so ravaged and traumatised by the abuse she suffered and the neglect of her needs and emotions, that even when she found sanctuary first via a local rescue centre and then coming to us, it was too late to repair the damage and although her spirit had returned and wished to stay, her physical body had failed beyond recovery. If love could have saved them both, we would have a herd of twelve now not ten. This has to be one of the hardest lessons we can learn.

Sometimes too, although the outcome may not be so devastating the journey can be a real roller-coaster ride that can cause us to doubt and question everything we thought we knew.

One of our herd, Sky has taken a long time to adapt and recover from a previous life and has caused me many a sleepless night wondering what else I can do, what I'm doing wrong and whether I really have a clue what I'm doing at all! You'll see in later chapters that this is all part of her story and our story together but she has also reminded me that even at our lowest moments, there is always a light and that actually letting go of all of those emotions is in fact exactly what needs to happen as part of the process.

On the 1st February 2014, she taught me that lesson......

"Today I cried. In fact I sobbed my heart out. I can feel the tears coming again as I'm writing this. As you know, the

constant wet weather is really starting to take its toll and Sky, our stunning TB mare has been feeling it the most, suffering with rainscald and dropping weight. I have found myself getting quite upset especially when I've arrived at the field to see several of the ponies shivering and cold, despite plenty of hay and rugs as needed and these are ponies who have lived out for years. Apparently we are experiencing the wettest January since 1767!!!

We have a brief interlude today where the sun came out, so I grabbed everyone's rugs off to allow them to feel the sun's warmth on their skin and be 'free' for a few hours and I spent some time with Sky, giving her a groom and assessing where her rainscald's at.......and that's when I sobbed.

As I groomed her, her hair came out in handfuls, leaving some bald patches and some sore open patches - she bent her body into me as I pulled out clump after clump from her back and bottom...and then I just broke down....all of a sudden I felt completely exhausted and as if I'd let her and the herd down....I couldn't hold it back any longer and I fell against her side and the tears fell.

As Sky realised I'd stopped brushing and grooming, she turned her head to me, saw my tears and shifted her body slightly so that she could wrap her head and neck around my body and she simply hugged me.... so gently but so completely.... and she let me cry into her chest until my tears stopped. Despite her skin being sore, her hair falling out, her legs and body having to be tired from the constant wet and mud - she thought of me and wanted to make me feel ok again!

I cannot describe the bond I feel with our beautiful, spiritual Sky - I have a different bond with all of the horses and ponies in the herd for example, Stanley is absolutely my soul horse and Gizmo makes me look at situations through his eyes....but with Sky it's something different, something unique - she knows me and knows how to help me 'let go' and that's no easy task - I am still struggling with my emotions relating to the boys and girls and the weather but Sky taught me today, *that that's ok - sometimes the best thing to do is let the tears flow, especially if you are being held by a 16.3hh stunningly beautiful TB mare called Sky"*

Trusting The Journey

As I talked about in the last chapter, sometimes the journey can be a rough one or it can simply seem to stall at a crossroads or a metaphorical 'layby' and we feel stuck, confused and frustrated. I have learned that often when that happens, it can be exactly what is supposed to be happening and we are exactly where we are supposed to be, as this experience on the 14th April 2015 reminded me.....

"I had a bit of an emotional experience tonight at the field. I have a lot going on at the moment personally, lots of 'where are I going?'....'what am I supposed to be doing?' and 'How can I possibly be doing it?' type stuff.

The difficulty for me is I know the answers to the questions, it's just that 'life' always seem to get in the way, usually involving money in one way or another and I keep getting stuck between who I really am/should be and the person I am in my 'daily life' of working and doing all those normal everyday type things.

Don't worry I'm not going to bore you with details.....I just needed to give you a little bit of background so the following experience makes sense.

It was a beautiful evening and after checking everyone and feeding supplements etc as necessary, I found myself sitting in the middle of the field, sharing space and breathe with Gizmo, Casper and Stanley in turn. I always love these moments and they remind me how very lucky I am.

As I was sitting watching Stan graze nearby and enjoying the sun slowly dipping in the sky, I found myself placing both hands on the nearly appearing grass, closing my eyes and asking Mother Nature to guide me, share her strength with me, support and advise me if she could about all of the questions and struggles running through my head. It just felt right so I went with it, feeling slightly 'spacey' as I did so.

As I opened my eyes, I had an urge to walk across the field to the little woods where we spread Squidge's ashes and as I did, I suddenly became aware that there were literally hundreds of little white feathers all over the field. Now I know the birds are doing their own version of shedding too at this time of year and these were all soft downy feathers but feathers also have significance so I also smiled as I received the message of being surrounded by angels, something I often feel when with our herd.

As I entered the quiet and coolness of the woods and went to visit with Squidge and say Hi, I noticed several grey feathers, larger ones this time, laying in various places. OK so now I was being given the message that 'yes life has been chaotic and stressful but peace is soon arriving'. I smiled as I connected with my favourite tree and then followed my

'feeling' out of the other entrance of the woods and around to where we have planted some of the willows. There lying next to the willows were two black and white feathers.....

At this point I felt a bit choked.....now I knew this was my answer to the request I had placed in the field. This part of the message was saying 'change is coming' and I felt at that moment very peaceful and basically 'OK'.

I wandered slowly back across the field, checking in with everyone as I did, smiling and feeling deeply honoured at such a strong and immediate response to my request. As I locked the shed and made my way to the car, I just 'felt' the words "Trust the journey, honour the experiences" and suddenly I realised that all of the questions and struggles and frustrations I am having are necessary for me to grow and be where I need to be, to be ready and able for whatever tomorrow brings.

It is hard sometimes to not be able to just 'be' where you want to be and to have to travel in a seemingly opposite direction but tonight I was reminded to 'enjoy the journey' and trust it, rather than be fixated on the destination.

I know things will be OK, I have no idea how or in what way and absolutely no clue what tomorrow will bring but tonight I was reminded of the amazing 'family' (human and non-human) and magical spaces I have and how if I trust in that, I will be exactly where I need to be and that will be just right.......and I am grateful for every step along the way."

A Case Of Mistaken Identity

Have you ever had the experience of judging someone or something by a previous person or experience? In reality, we do it all the time; it's part of human psychology but here I'm talking about actually 'loading' an innocent individual with the negative emotions and thoughts you collected through the interactions with another individual.

As I said, it's a part of human psychology to short-cut things like this and use our previous knowledge, information or experiences to make sense of new ones. It only becomes a problem really when that experience was unbalanced, discriminatory or emotionally charged and that then 'colours' our new experiences with different individuals.

Due to the work I do (teaching) I often perhaps arrogantly, pride myself of being aware of this in my interactions with people and horses, especially as stereotypes and discrimination is still sadly prevalent for both. That's why the realisation that I have been loading Sky with my fears and guilt from a previous life came as such a shock...but it was to be a valuable and well learnt lesson!

"When you judge another, you do not define them, you define yourself" (Dr Wayne Dyer)

On 14th September 2012 this happened....

"I thought I would share this with you as it seems very appropriate for our journey – I always look forward to reading the 'daily posts' from Seven Acre Horse Sanctuary and this was this morning's post....

"Thought 4the day: We are not here just to heal horses... horses are also here to heal us. We all have our own 'quirks' and 'issues' just like our four legged friends. I prefer to call it baggage as everyone gets some at some point in life and so

67

do equines. We may feel that we have nothing wrong at some point yet have you ever thought why? Horses mirror image us when one, they know us better than we do and you may never notice they heal you. Love them, cherish them, respect them and always listen to them."

Very true words and anyone who has taken the time to really understand and 'listen' to horses will be nodding now ....but what was more significant about this post today was that it was as if they had read my mind!!

Here is my reply to show you why....."Have you been reading my mind this morning!!!?? Was only talking about this with Darren yesterday and how I've now realised that the beautiful Sky has come into my life (at least) to enable me to confront and let go of an unresolved fear I had (and had forgotten about completely!!) of a TB mare from years ago!!!

You see I couldn't work out why I was being so 'super-cautious' around her then (tonne of bricks dropping!!!) I remembered....so we had a good long chat yesterday - myself and Sky-bo - and we have agreed to 'practice' trusting each other every day and not expecting and anticipating pain/fear or anxiety and she will let me know when I need a reminder - hopefully we will both 'lose some baggage' as we move forward.

(Bizarrely the mare I loved but was terrified of years ago, was nick-named Baggage because of her issues - weird but true!!) - I love this post and I love horses for being able to show us how to be better people xx"

Now 'Baggage' or Carrie as she was officially known was a 15.3hh 18 year old TB mare I met while learning about horses many years ago, she had been mistreated over her life and was very defensive, including kicking and biting if she felt threatened. I was not experienced enough and hadn't come nearly far enough on my 'journey' to understand or even comprehend where she was at in her mind and to cut a long story short, although I loved her as I love all of the animals that enter my life, I never truly trusted her and we were both as afraid and defensive as each other (we never hurt each other, we just didn't trust). Eventually she went to a new home but I've always felt guilt about it and it seems, have always carried that fear I felt with me (I think it's more a fear of not being good enough – not as a rider but as a trusted and valued partner to a horse, as someone who will be there to stand up for them and do what it takes to ensure their happiness and comfort, if that makes sense??)

I often wondered what happened to Baggage and will never know but now I believe that Sky may be here to help me continue and resolve that part of my journey, at a time when I am more ready to learn the lessons that she (and Baggage) have to teach…."

Since that day Sky has been a mirror for my fears and emotions many times but now we can work with them together and in honesty without holding unnecessary 'history'. Interestingly she has reminded me of this lesson again very recently. As you will read through this book, she has been through a lot of changes, particularly physical ones and I hadn't realised that slowly over a long period of time, I had come to see her as ill and broken; needing fixing. Again in the way only she can, she explained that if only I would stop projecting my negative energy about her supposed lack of health, she could actually get on with the business of healing herself!!

"Whether you think you can or think you can't,
you're right" (Henry Ford)

"All that we are is a result of all that we have thought"
(Buddha)

Sometimes A Hug Is all You Need

There are times when for whatever reason, we simply need to be 'hugged' - nothing more. We don't need fixing or to receive advice at those moments, just to simply be held while we breathe and find balance again. Over the years, our herd and the horses and ponies I have had the pleasure to meet have shown me this truth more times that I can remember. There have been so many times when I thought I was fine, maybe a little stressed but coping or when I had my priorities all messed up and was running around trying to do a million things at once and one or another of the ponies would simply place themselves in my path and gently but firmly make me stop 'for a cuddle' (even when I thought I didn't want one!)

"Someday, someone is going to hug you so tight that all of your broken pieces will stick back together"
(Unknown)

Allowing ourselves to be 'held' (and often healed) either physically or metaphorically for a while is a gift we shouldn't ever turn away from, particularly if that gift is being presented by someone who loves you unconditionally and knows what it is to 'hold space' for you; something our horses and other animals are experts at.

Here are two recent pieces I wrote about exactly this lesson….the first from February 19th 2014

"I am off on leave this week and seem to have chosen the best week, in terms of the weather. I have been able to spend some real quality time with the herd, that hasn't involved slopping through mud, being battered by gale force winds and getting soaked through to the skin with constant and torrential rain.

One of my 'duties' this week has been defined by our beautiful Sky - I must spend at least 45 minutes a day grooming, scratching, rubbing, massaging, creaming and generally cuddling our gorgeous dark fluffy girl!!! The photo below shows what happens when I get to the field......"I'm coming Mum, get the brushes and stuff ready..." It seems she has the herd's approval too as no one interferes with our 'together time' until she is happy and has had enough. Bearing in mind she isn't a high ranking member in terms of RHP (resource holding potential) so could be chased away by at least four other members should they chose to, this seems to be a reasonable and certainly interesting conclusion.

What makes it even more fascinating is that as soon as she's had enough for one 'session' and we can have several sessions a day, she will give me a nudge and wander off and whoever the herd has decided is next will wander over for their 'cuddle time'. Most of the time I don't even move, they take it in turns to come to me!

Sky has also perfected her 'cuddling' technique too during our time together..... Not all of the herd do it, but several members have a very distinct 'cuddling' method which usually involves hooking their heads over your shoulder and pulling you into their chests - Flash, Willow and Stanley are particularly good at it (Red normally just cuddles you with his bottom which is whole different thing but that's him) and now Sky has given it a her own unique and heart-melting twist.......she wraps her head and neck over your shoulder and down around your back, literally like she using her head and neck like an arm, and gently but firmly tucks you into her shoulder, with your face snuggled into her incredibly velvety neck - yes I was

completely 'soppy' after our cuddle today and wandered around with a very silly smile on my face for quite some time!!

I am so grateful of the time I have to be with our herd-family at the moment - I think it's what we've all needed after such an awful, long and grey winter - we are able to help each other rejuvenate, relax and rest in preparation for Spring…."

…and again on the 30th April 2014…..

"Our wonderful Toffee, the Shetland, gave me the most amazing cuddle tonight.

I was watching the herd moving and interacting around the track, which I love doing and eventually the herd gathered together and set off down the track towards to the far end, so I thought "Ok that's a good point for me to head home".

Just as I was about to head off, Toffee wandered over to me (rather than go with the herd) and asked for a cuddle, which of course I happily obliged him with......well, before I knew it, half an hour had gone past and I was sitting on the track with

Toffee standing over my legs, breathing rhythmically into my ear...both of us with our eyes closed and just barely touching each other, although it felt like we were totally connected, almost outside of time.....and then, when he felt it was time, he breathed a deep sigh, stretched and carefully stepped over me to wander off with his 'family' who by now were half way down the track.

I could analyse what and why...but I'm not going to because it doesn't need to be analysed...just accepted in the loving spirit in which Toffee gave me this moment as a gift and for that I am simply and completely grateful."

As I say in that last piece, moments like this remind me to be grateful for everything I have, everything I am and everything I have experienced in my lifetime. Actually gratitude is something which has become a large part of my life in recent years. When we are grateful for every moment and look for the gifts we are given, our lives become fuller and happier, allowing us to cope with tough times and appreciate wonderful times.

"We are most alive when our hearts are conscious of our treasures" (Thornton Wilder)

Sometimes as I've mentioned, by changing our focus, not dwelling on sadness and fear but being grateful it can help us through the most difficult of times.

I remember looking down at Squidge, our little Jack Russell girl, cuddled into my arms and knowing she was leaving (her body was failing and was no longer strong enough to contain her beautiful spirit) and despite feeling so very sad that this would be one of the last cuddles I would have with her, also being so grateful for that moment and for all the years we had shared. This was also where having learnt to 'feel' fully and deeply allowed me to be truly appreciate the moment and create a unique memory of it, so that whenever I miss her I can close my eyes and 'feel' that cuddle all over again.

More recently, I have experienced sitting with the puppies on my lap sleeping curled around each other, feeling them breathe and just being filled with such gratitude and love, it felt like I almost couldn't contain it. I have been enjoying an impromptu hug from one of the herd and suddenly noticed the most incredible sunset that I might have missed if not for a pony deciding I needed that hug and I have found space to cry and release pent up emotions in the embrace of the warm, soft neck of one of the herd.

So, allow yourself to be held from time to time and before you go to sleep each night, take a moment to find at least one thing to be thankful for. You may have had an awful day, where everything went wrong but there will always be something to be grateful for so really try to find that thing and acknowledge it. Doing this changes your mind-set which is particularly beneficial if you're trying to get to sleep and the more you practice 'gratitude, the more you will find to be thankful for.

Life Is For Living

One of the most important things I have learned from our horses is always, always keep a sense of humour. There are always going to be rough days and tough times and for the most part there may be little we can do bar 'ride the storm' and keep going until things get better.

It is the cycle of life and without the tough and difficult times we would not be able to appreciate the good times when they come.

"A person without a sense of humour is like a wagon without springs, it's jolted by every pebble on the road"
(Henry Ward Beecher)

"Laugh often; Laugh longest" **(Sky)**

Here's a funny reminder of that from Casper from 14th June 2014…

"Had to giggle today. I've had this strange little urge for a couple of days to sit in Casper (bareback of course) and he's been very attentive for some time now.

Today while I was doing the waters, the little urge appeared again and I quietly went and got my hat and a leadrope to use as a cordeo.

Casper stood while I popped the 'cordeo' on and put my hat on, he also stood while I leant right over his back and jumped and down next to him (he is backed and a lovely horse to ride but this is a whole different ball-game!)

Then as Darren was stroking him I attempted to 'get on'....Hmmmm well let's just say when you get to your 40's your bounce isn't quite as 'bouncy' - Casper bless him still stood - bear in mind he wasn't restricted at all and wasn't being held onto.

As I slithered down his rather rotund belly for the second time and he just stood looking back at me, I laughingly said to him "Maybe Mum isn't quite as committed to this as she thinks eh Casp!!" Darren came round to give me a leg-up laughing and as he took my knee and went to lift me........Casper walked away!!!! He stopped a few steps away and looked back as if to say "if you're not up for it, that's fine...we'll do it another day but let's not make a mess of it today"

Both myself and Darren just stood laughing at the look on his face and the fact we were standing in the middle of the field with Darren holding my leg in mid-air and me with my arms in front of me, resting on a pony who was no longer there!!!

The lesson for today is.......trust your horse and trust yourself and if you are going to try a new activity, for your horses sake, commit to it 100%.....oh and get a mounting block!!"

Something else I have learned is that life should be experienced, not watched and every day should be seen as if we were a child waking up in a magical world of possibilities and adventures!

OK, that might seem a bit far-fetched especially when we all have bills to pay and responsibilities to honour. The key though is not to let those things define your life and take it over.

"Some people feel the rain. Others just get wet"
(Bob Marley)

As you may now be understanding, there is magic everywhere if we open our eyes and even the simplest things and craziest days can bring magic and adventures when we chose to live each day instead of simply functioning.

For example, when was the last time you stepped out into a wide open space and just danced or jumped or ran......for no reason, just because it felt good to feel the wind on your face and feel your body moving?

"And those who were seen dancing were thought to be insane by those who could not hear the music."
(Friedrich Nietzsche)

Horses have taught me to feel joy in a 'loud', physical way and to wear myself out,   Our bodies need to feel physical tiredness, in the same way as horses NEED to gallop from time to time and be free to explode with energy when they need to.

We need to play too! Even as we grow up and become adults, the need for play and fun and expressing ourselves in a creative and physical way doesn't leave us, although it is often suppressed. It is interesting that recent research is starting to illustrate how play and creativity and fun are vital for our mental, psychological and physical health, something our horses and the rest of the animal kingdom knew all along!

"We don't stop playing because we grow old; we grow old because we stop playing." (George Bernard Shaw)

81

There's Magic Everywhere!

When we are children, magic exists everywhere. Then somehow as we get older, we seem to lose the ability to see it and very quickly convince ourselves that it is a 'childish' thing, partly due to the way the adult world works and partly because the education most of us receive provides us with seemingly convincing evidence that what we previously thought of as magic is easily explained away by science, technology and theory.

"Those who don't believe in magic will never find it"
(Roald Dahl)

What if I told you the magic still exists and you can find it wherever you need to – in fact, right now if you could if you wanted to!

If we look around and learn to appreciate and really 'see' things not just as a part of the whirl of our everyday lives but as beautiful and unique, then suddenly the magic we knew existed as a child returns to us. Suddenly every morning is the start of something new and inspiring and in any given moment, we can close our eyes and open them again to see the world around us in a different way.

I have learnt through our herd to see beyond what my eyes see and to see with my heart and in doing so, I have been introduced to a whole new world. A world where everything is connected and our thoughts can bring our dreams to life; a world where energy is not just the stuff that runs through cables in our homes…it's all around us and within us and we can communicate and heal through it.

What is interesting is that our animals have even taught me how to use that energy and work within it……

"I was sitting at home the other day, day dreaming with our two puppies on my lap and thinking about the herd in an absent-minded way. Without realizing it, I found myself seeing the answer to my personal question of how I can use and share the energy within the universe and everything around us.

As I have learned and grown, I have come to realise that there is an energy that is within and around all of us and everything within this world and within the universe. That isn't me going a bit weird, it's a proven scientific fact. The difficulties come when people try to define and explain this energy and how it affects us all. It gets even more complicated when we start talking about chakra's and how we can use this energy to help and heal and see and communicate with the world around us.

For me personally, despite the fact I know and can feel the energy, I am at the very beginning of my journey in understanding it. I found myself getting confused and tied up in the how's and when's and trying to perfect techniques, that those more expert in this field have tried to teach me, much like I used to do in my interactions with our horses and ponies. The times when I have felt the energy most strongly it has come from different places e.g. sometimes through my feet from the earth, sometimes from above and sometimes from the trees, air and animals around me. Then during the times I have been able to share that energy with an animal or person or even the environment around me i.e. give it back as healing and love, it felt as if it came straight from me.

I kept thinking "Am I doing this wrong?"...."Am I creating problems for those I share with?" ....so many doubts because for me it didn't seem to 'work' the way everyone was telling me it should or should I say the way I was 'interpreting' the way people were telling me it should!

Then, during this day dream I saw the answer or what I believe the animals in my life were trying to show as the answer for me about interacting and sharing 'the magic'.

I saw myself standing in the middle of our field with my arms open to my sides and my eyes closed. At the height of my chest was a huge glowing ball of light spinning and sending light outwards in all directions and I was aware that this was an image of me 'recharging my batteries' so to speak from the world and universe around me – all around me...the earth, the sky, the environment...everywhere.

Then as soon as I accepted this image and the message it sent, it changed to show me giving that light back to the animals and people around me when it was needed, whenever it was needed, in whatever way was right for that moment.

Now I don't know whether that 'way' fits the textbooks but then I've never been too good at that and neither have our horses and ponies; I do know though that in that moment it all made complete sense to me and the parts which had been confused and concerned me before, no longer do. For me, it seems that I can 'recharge' through nature and store that love and 'energy' within me to share as needed. Suddenly it became so simple and didn't scare me so much anymore.

I have struggled with that for several years, believing I should do this or that to get it right. The problem was I forgot to simply believe and just let the magic (the energy) flow!"

I'm pretty convinced that that image was 'sent' by one of the herd (it's happened many times before).

We are lucky to have a piece of woodland at the field, only a small area but it has such 'magic' within it that I will often simply go and walk beneath the trees and touch the branches. I might get a feeling if I'm sitting in the field and it's as if the woodland is calling me so I have learnt to follow that request and often, I will find something or see something or just resolve a problem simply by being there, that I would not have if I hadn't. Other people have visited our woodland (and field) and have said they get a similar feeling. That's the reason we scattered Squidge's ashes under one of the oak trees there so she could become a part of the magic (in truth I know she already was) and if ever we are 'gifted' a message in the form of orbs or lights from our other beautiful girls, Annie, Cindy, Puzzle and Wilber now in spirit, they will appear around the woods.

When we let go of our restrictive and limiting beliefs, the world becomes once again the magical place it was when we were young and in fact, always has been, if only we had remained open....

Everything You Need Is Inside Of You

By far the greatest lesson that I have learned from our herd and in particular from Stanley, Gizmo and Willow is to be myself and more importantly, to honour and respect all that this is.

For far too long I struggled with acceptance of the parts of myself that I didn't actually like very much; the parts that made me feel guilt or regret and the parts that scared me more than a little.

I have done things in the past that I don't like thinking about and wouldn't do now (haven't we all!) and I have always struggled with acceptance of that side of me, especially now I have learnt how powerful thoughts and emotions can be. It has been through the acceptance and unconditional love of the herd and through watching their interactions with others that I am slowly learning to accept and be comfortable with those parts of myself.

For some time it felt that every time I thought I had 'found myself', my inner strength, my pure and positive light and belief in who I was, I would be swamped with external stimuli that seemed to trigger negativity and anger...even rage...inside of me. Much of this external 'prodding' came from what was happening in the animal world around me and filled me with such confusion and exhaustion at trying to remain positive and giving, when all I actually wanted to do was give Karma a helping hand and physically hurt someone in revenge for the hurt and pain they were causing others!! Scary!

At first, every time it happened I believed it was a 'test'; some kind of challenge that I had to overcome in order to become a better person and know I could resist the 'dark side' so to speak.

In fact by doing so, I was missing the message entirely!

Yet again, it has been the herd and the horses and animals that I came in contact with, that gently and quietly showed me what I should have been learning from the experiences.

"The darkest nights produce the brightest stars"
(unknown)

There is a balance in everything and we cannot have positive without negative otherwise how can we know what positive is?

"The dark does not destroy the light; it defines it. It's our fear of the dark that casts our joy into the shadows"
(Brene Brown)

It can be called many things... Yin and yang, good and evil, up and down, black and white... however we choose to describe it, we need balance and to have balance we need both elements.

By understanding that lesson we can begin to believe in ourselves and be true to ourselves instead of trying to be what we believe society, our friends, our families or whoever believes we should be.

"To remember who you are, you need to forget who they told you to be" (unknown)

This too, has been a huge lesson for me to learn and is one that I try to pass on whenever I can. You see, if you believe in yourself and have confidence in yourself, you won't be so easily 'beaten down' by negativity and those times when life doesn't quite go according to plan.

Trust your instincts, understand that nobody is perfect, it's ok to be vulnerable as long as you are coming from a place of authenticity. Try entering a field with a herd of horses who you want to interact with and doing it while 'hiding' your true self, your emotions or fears. You will likely get one of a few reactions dependent on the horses involved...including moving as far away as possible, being seemingly very 'in your space' and 'demanding' (in order to cause you to take notice of your behaviour) or simply not being very interested or responsive. Horses and the animals around us will quickly remind us when we are being fake, even when we don't believe we are!

From a place of self-love, balanced self-belief and authenticity, we can achieve pretty much anything we want to and at the same time accept and respect those things that challenge us by seeing them as lessons and opportunities for growth and development.

"A bird sitting on a tree is never afraid of the branch breaking, because its trust is not in the branch but in its own wings" (unknown)

There was a time not so very long ago when I honestly believed that although I could always ensure my horses had as natural and happy a life as I could give them, I did not have the 'power' or knowledge to take it any further than that. Yet again it was the horses and ponies who became a part of my life that were to teach me how wrong I was.

Over the years I have watched seemingly smaller, weaker or less dominant horses and ponies achieve incredible things, both with their herds and families and also with their humans. I have watched and read about situations where horses and humans have become tangled in a struggle of confusion and fear and then seen or heard about one person or one horse appearing at the right time and bringing peace and calm to what seemed a lost situation.

Within our own herd, both Gizmo and Little Sky have shown that with determination, respect, good communcation and just the right amount of courage, you can eat from the best piles of hay or share a mutual groom with all members of the herd.

I have watched Gizmo, our 9hh New Forest put this lesson into practice many many times and through his patience and precise reading of a situation, he has created a life for himself that suits him and places him in a very well respected position in the herd.

Never doubt that one individual can make a difference!

If I hadn't met Annie at the sanctuary open day all those years ago, I would never have considered making the changes and putting in the effort that I did in order to give her a forever home. Although the universe had other plans for her and she was called home before she could come to us, the significance of the few weeks I knew her will never be forgotten. She changed things for me and for the herd and for everything else that came afterwards and I cannot thank her enough for sharing that gift with me. She is and always will be my 'Golden Girl' and she showed me where and how to 'find my power' and create something more special and important than I had ever dreamed of.

However, part of 'finding your power' so to speak is to learn humilty with it.

"Be humble for you are made of earth, be noble for you are made of stars" (Serbian proverb)

When I talk about being humble here, I don't mean being meek and subservient – horses don't think like that. I am referring to the meaning of humble which encompasses being unpretentious and respectful; basically the opposite of arrogance.

I see a lot of arrogance around me, both in the horse world (a lot!!) and in everyday life. There seems to be a very negative trend towards one-upmanship and proving you're the best by putting everyone else down or showing them up.

When I first started wanting to make a difference in the horse world, after the initial "who the hell do I think I am?" phase, I found myself getting into the same 'game' of trying to convince people of the correctness of my way by picking apart, discrediting and generally talking very negatively about other ways that didn't sit well with me. That's all well and good but all that does is alienate people and push them even further away. Sadly it is often then the horses that suffer even more as those people become even more entrenched in and committed to the methods they may be using simply because you have attacked them!

For example, let's consider the bitless 'debate' in the horse world. After years of riding using a bit but something nagging me about it, then researching and reading and learning just how painful and abusive these devices actually are, I am a firm believer in riding bitless for ANY horse now – I make no apologies for that.

Until very recently I would quite literally state these facts as I saw them to anyone considering riding a horse with a bit and I couldn't understand how anyone with an ounce of compassion or sense could disagree with my passionately argued case. How wrong was I? I had let my arrogance cloud my respect of another's choices and in doing so had achieved the exact opposite of what I had set out to do. I hadn't changed anything for the better for horse or rider, maybe even made it worse, and I had simply wound myself in the process!

Above all else, I had forgotten that I too had travelled that route not so very long ago and if someone had come to me then and made me feel small and foolish or told me I was cruel and selfish for riding with a bit when I knew no better, how would I have felt? It is human nature to protect ourselves even if that means we disregard important and logical information because the person delivering it made us feel terrible and belittled.

Now, of course, I'm not saying don't stand up for what you believe or know is right – what I am saying is there is a right way and wrong way to get that message across. Horses know that and are masters at communicating within their herds and families. It's about knowing 'when to advance and when to retreat' - something that Gizmo and Little Sky are expert at. It's about knowing how far to push while respecting the other individual, their feelings and where they are at. It's about knowing when to walk away for the benefit of everyone involved and when to stand your ground and most importantly it's about doing these things for the right reasons and not for some egocentric need to be right or prove a point.

Learning Naturally...

Just outside our comfort zone is where the magic happens – the trick is not to step too far and find fear while missing the magic. That in itself is a very delicate balancing act but we should never be afraid to try something new!

We have learned over the years that the very best way to 'teach' any of the herd something new is to allow them to teach themselves if at all possible. In other words set the situation up so that they can 'test things out' or have a look in a very relaxed way and in their own time.

Another thing we always do is do everything we can at liberty – it is interesting that when there is the opportunity to leave, if you have spent time building the relationship and trust, our herd members will often choose to stay even when they are anxious or unsure! Let's be honest the same would apply to us too – if we are given the opportunity to do something scary or learn something new in a safe environment with people we trust and we weren't being forced, the chances are we'd give it a go and see, despite feeling worried or nervous. Force us to do something that is a challenge and at the very least we probably won't learn anything very well and at worst we may develop a phobia, avoid that situation altogether in the future or even get hurt.

Here's an example of what I mean.....

5th March 2012

"I watched an amazing bit of 'learning' and 'building courage' in my ponies over the weekend (and I didn't really do a thing!). I had hung their hay in haynets on the end fencing as it was so wet and windy and I wanted them to have a little bit of shelter while they were eating. The woods on the other side of the fence lead down to a railway track and as it was Sunday, they were obviously doing some work on the track as there was lots of loud banging, roaring and what sounded like very heavy machinery going up and down the track right behind us! The 'boys' couldn't see through the woods what was making the noise and initially, every time there was a crash, roar or bang, they would all react instinctively and as a herd, spin round and gallop about half way up the field!! Completely normal behaviour. What was so interesting though was each time it happened, they shortened the distance they 'fled' until

eventually and within only about 15 minutes, they didn't budge at all!! In that very short space of time, as a herd, they had realised and 'worked out' that whatever the sound was, it wasn't going to 'get them' so there was no need to worry anymore. Amazing! They learnt safely as a herd and were able to act out their normal behaviours appropriately so the situation was dealt with extremely quickly, with very little stress and no injuries or panicking and I didn't do a thing!

This is why I keep my ponies as I do (or at least one of the reasons anyway)! The whole herd also now have more trust, courage and strength in themselves and each other – Fantastic!!"

"If you want something you've never had, you must be willing to do something you've never done" (Thomas Jefferson)

We have also learned to seize any opportunity for learning, particularly if it is accompanies by a sense of curiosity.

"I have no special talents, I am only passionately curious" (Albert Einstein)

If it hadn't been for the insatiable curiosity of Willow when he was a foal we may never have been able to show 'the babies' as they were known then that we were safe and wouldn't hurt them.

So, never stop being curious, ask questions and never stop
learning……….

"Millions saw the apple fall, only Newton asked why"
(Bernard Baruch)

Breathing isn't Optional!

"You are where you need to be. Just breathe"

Stanley taught me to breathe. I know that sounds ridiculous doesn't it! I don't mean the type of breathing that starts the moment we are born and stops the moment we transition to spirit, I mean the type of breathing that connects us with ourselves, nature and the planet around us; the type of deep, slow healing breathe that grounds us where we are and allows us to clear our minds and simply be.

Learning how to breathe has enabled me to help Casper (and other horses since) when he found himself separated from the herd and feeling quite anxious on January 18th 2014......

"Have you ever tried breathing with your horse?

We do, quite often, when we are spending time quietly with a member or two of the herd and it's incredibly relaxing and peaceful, as well as allowing a meditative state, which is something I struggle to achieve anywhere else. Yes, yet again, our horses are teaching me what I need to know to take the next step in our journey.

Yesterday though I also experimented with using breathe energy to calm an excited Casper down.....you see, Toffee and Whipper had got through to the top paddock, Sky had broken into the front wood paddock and Casper...well he was on the track!! Sky, as soon as she saw us, made her way back and Darren simply opened the gate and let her in (she knew her tea was waiting and she wasn't about to miss out).

As Casper was on the track, we decided to pop a headcollar on him and lead him into and through the field that Toffee and Whipper were in so we could 'pick them up' on the way and walk them all back to the winter paddock and their hay. Well, Casper was fine till we started walking away from the herd, and then when we went through the gate into a different paddock, he grew about 6 inches and turned into a kangaroo, bouncing about on his toes (hooves)

Instead of reprimanding him for his 'bad manners' which I know some would do, I simply continued walking in the direction we were wanting to go, ensuring the leadrope stayed loose, keeping my voice monotone, quiet and low as I asked him to calm his energy down for me and breathe with me, so that we could both get where we needed to go.....now this is Casper who gets excited at the thought of getting excited...but even I was a little surprised when he looked at me, looked at the field and the herd, looked back at me, lowered his head, levelled himself with me and walked calmly across the field !!! The power of connection through breathe – amazing"

"You don't always need a plan. Sometimes you just need to breathe, trust, let go and see what happens"
(Mandy Hale)

Don't Forget To Stop & Smell The Roses

Our lives are so fast paced and filled with commitments usually that often we can miss positive opportunities completely or are simply not paying attention enough to even notice that they are there. That's sad and especially when you consider that life is relatively short and we only get one shot at this one. Life itself is an opportunity and one we should be grasping with both hands and clinging on to.

Have you ever had those moments when time has passed and you have no idea where it went or what you did – I don't mean suffering from some kind of amnesia...it's those moments, perhaps driving home on a familiar route when you suddenly realise you ten or twenty miles further than where you last acknowledged you were and you honestly don't remember it.

When was the last time you truly felt the rain on your face and appreciated the smell of the raindrops on wet grass? When was the last time you stopped and experienced something with every sense you have, fully, deeply and completely?

The 15th October 2013 was just such a moment....

"Have you ever had a moment of such pure happiness, it overwhelmed you? I have been lucky enough to have a few in my lifetime and they have all been while I was with horses and other animals. Last night I was gifted another incredibly special moment by the boys and girls and the beauty of nature.

As usual I was at the field after work (1st job), feeding, haying and generally checking everyone was ok before heading off to my 2nd job (teaching adult ed evening classes) and was a little frustrated that it meant I had to 'rush through' my time with the herd in order to 'get to work'.

Everyone had had their feed, Sky seemed better and appears to be gaining a few pounds slowly but surely and I had spread the hay out in loads of small piles so they could move and play and chase each other or whatever they wanted to do. I was tidying the bowls and thinking "great – all done....I can get going with plenty of time for traffic allowances ..." when the universe put the brakes on for me....and boy am I glad!!!!

I turned to walk back across the field at exactly the moment the sun broke through some cloud and being low in the evening sky, literally stopped me in my tracks as I was momentarily blinded. As the brilliant light slowly paled to a more 'manageable' hue, my eyes slowly focused and were rewarded with the most beautiful sunset - shafts of lights cast across the whole field. I turned back to look at the herd as the sunlight lit up the area of field they were in as if setting them on a stage in the spotlight....and was given such a rush of joy, pure love and happiness – I honestly can't find words beautiful enough to do it justice.

I couldn't move – it was such a spiritual moment and I was completely lost in the positive energy….for those few moments I felt what it was like to be part of the herd and feel their love for each other, their contentment and their joy at being alive.

As the moment slowly passed (several minutes having gone by) I was left in a state of complete peace and gratitude at being allowed to share such a deep and moving experience…….so much so…I cried with happiness most of the way to 'work'…….even now as I write this, the emotion is so strong – I am so lucky to be able to share my life with such special souls in such a beautiful place."

"Stop for a minute…."

I am the world's worst at 'being still' so I've discovered! I didn't actually know I was until I tried to 'not do anything'. It was physically uncomfortable and mentally frustrating and that came as a bit of a shock to me.

When I actually thought about it, I realised that I rarely just sit still, at home, at work, with the horses….in fact anywhere. I am always either physically doing something that I believe needs doing or my mind is mulling something over or working something out. No wonder I'm so exhausted so much of the time! Does that sound familiar? I bet it does.

Sadly the world many of us live in causes us to become this way without us even realising it and before we know it, our lives are ebbing away in flurry of alarm calls, work deadlines, family commitments and paying bills.

On the 8th December 2013, I wrote an entry on our Facebook Page because the herd had just reminded me of this lesson......

"As you will know, The Free Spirit Ponies project is about helping people to help their horses and develop relationships that bring out the best for both....sometimes however, that means I get so passionate and caught up with sharing information, helping horses and their people and 'spreading the word', that I don't give The Free Spirit Ponies the time they need with me too.

Today I was due to be taking one of the sanctuary horses to a clear round jumping, bitless of course , to get him out and about and help him find his forever home but I kept getting a nagging feeling that my 'herd' needed me. Right up until this morning, I kept 'pushing the nagging feeling' aside as I'd made a commitment to the sanctuary......but when I woke up, I couldn't shake it – it was as if the boys and girls were 'calling' inside my head so I sent my profuse apologies to SAHS and Sam and headed off to the field.

Well, I had the most amazing day and experienced things I would have missed otherwise. The thing was, the herd didn't actually need me...but they knew I needed them....I needed to rest and re-group and 'ground myself' with those who knew me best. Apart from getting lots of little jobs done and discovering that Sky doesn't in fact have rainscald.....it's more like over-zealous grease/oil production (!!) that's caused the hair to 'clump' but there are no sores and the skin seems to be fine – I was able to have a really good look today as she let me know it was ok to give her a brush – I was given so much love by the herd I was able to completely relax (tough for me) and enjoy their 'gifts'.

For example, at one point Gizmo kept nudging me and as he is 'Shetland size' (physically only, not in his heart) I knelt down to see what he wanted and say Hi. He promptly put his head on top of my head and then pulled me into him and wrapped his head and neck around mine so I was 'snuggled' in his very soft and fluffy chest! That was the first time I nearly sobbed.....

The second time was a little later, when after enjoying his morning hay, Willow laid down and settled into a lovely snooze. I kept getting such a sense of peace so much so I even said it out loud, though there was no human to hear it. Something told me to go and sit with Willow, so I did and he closed his eyes and fell asleep next to me (see the picture). As I turned around grinning from ear to ear and feeling so happy and peaceful, Red ambled over and laid down with us and slowly one by one, the rest of the herd gathered and took their preferred 'dozing' positions, some laying down, some standing. Part of me wanted to cry out loud with the pure joy of it but the stillness of the moment kept me quiet, partly for fear of it ending but mostly because the herd knew that what I needed most was to 'stop, be still and breathe' and before I knew it, I was breathing in time with Willow, sleeping next to me.

I am so glad I 'listened' to the herd calling me today and because of them, as always, I am refreshed and empowered to continue our 'journey' having shed the 'stress' and everyday 'stuff' that had begun to blur my focus.......I am yet again indebted to our beautiful herd although I know they will have consider the debt paid the moment I sat down with them."

I needed another reminder on 30th July 2014.......

"I had planned to do a bit of a photo-shoot of all of the grasses and plants in our field tonight so that I could properly identify each of them but.......Stanley had other plans for me

As I walked over to check the water butts and repair a bit of fencing, he walked across the field to me and just stood in front of me - I started to wipe the flies from his face and give him a bit of a scratch but he twitched and swished his head away as if to say 'no I don't need you to do anything...just stand with me'....and so I did.

We stood for a long time together mostly in silence, although I did ask him if he was happy and ok and I felt his answer was yes. For some of the time we simply stood side by side, for some of the time we stood tucked into each other, Stan's head wrapped around my shoulder and neck and my arms wrapped around his, at his request and for some of the time, I laid my face against his neck and breathed deeply into his mane. Each time Stanley guided me to where he wished me to be and I followed his guidance...much of the time we closed our eyes together and it felt like we were connected as one

I don't know how long we stood but I do know that when it felt right we both breathed a huge deep sigh and slowly opened

117

our eyes - Stanley placed his forehead in my hand for a scratch and I, of course, obliged by tensing my fingers so he could scratch himself (which he prefers - I don't think I do it right for him) and when he had finished, I gave him a soft kiss on his neck, took a final deep breath into his mane to breathe in his his unique energy and presence, ran my hand over his forelock and he nudged me - then he wandered off back to his friends and, after checking in and saying to Hi to everyone else, I came home - relaxed, content, incredibly happy and at peace with the world....

Stanley has been in my life for 12 wonderful years, since he 'found' me (and I pray, many more) and he still knows me far better than I know myself"

....and again on 15th February 2015 (Like I said I'm the world's worst!!)

"Busy day today, moving the hay feeders to a slightly different position which drains better while Darren put an additional line of fencing along Wilber's paddock as Sky was eyeing up the new grass a bit too enthusiastically!!

Then just as I was going to start another job that needed doing, Gizmo walked out of the herd and away from his hay and made me stop and spend time with him. He isn't a particularly 'cuddly' pony but he does know exactly how and when to make you take 'time out' and just stop and think. I think he was feeling a little sad too as our friends next door had to say goodbye to their beloved stallion yesterday - a beautiful gentle and kind soul, who Gizmo seemed to feel a kindred spirit with. So we shared time, breathe and space for as long as he needed and felt we should. It was so very special as it always is when one of the herd takes time out to share with me.

I hadn't realised Darren had captured it on camera but I am grateful he did so I can share it with you too. Gizmo really is a very special spirit with a huge heart and a deep soul. Thank you Giz xx "

Being Patient with Healing

Back in July 2012, we welcomed two TB mares into our family. At the time we didn't know that Cindy, a beautiful ex-racehorse in her twenties had chosen us to allow her to know what it was like to just 'be a horse' for a while before she was called to transition to the next stage of her journey in the November of that year.

Sky, her friend and a much younger lady, however was about to take us on a journey that would challenge us so much, bring tears and a great deal of laughter but ultimately teach us that sometimes healing has to run its own course; that is the foundation of the process and although we can assist and support, we cannot force either a body or a mind to heal itself before it is ready, even if we have the most heartfelt and empathetic reasons for wishing to do so.

You've already met Sky in the chapter titled Holding Sky and although that experience was most definitely part of her journey, it warranted its own space in this book because it held a lesson all of its own.

Sky is a very special teacher. When I think of her the saying *"The best teachers are those who show you where to look but don't tell you what to see"* (Alexandra K Trenfor) springs to mind. I have had every belief and 'fact' I thought I knew tested as we have shared time and experiences in each other company (you will see she appears in another chapter too) and although there have been times I have felt despair and so ineffective a guardian for her, she always held me just above the point of no return – a point where I could shed ego-based and limiting beliefs and start again. That is a great gift.

She has taught me to be patient in a whole new way, not just for her but with all things; she has shown me that often it is better to look at the whole picture, rather than try to focus on a small part of it; she has taught me that I cannot 'fix' everything just because I want to or have the power to – some things have a course to run and that in itself is where the 'fixing' happens if it is supposed to and she has taught me that by 'holding space' for her and listening to her, even when those around me might be saying "do this, do that, she needs blah blah..." together we can grow and become the incredible beings we could have and were always capable of being.

On 24th August 2013, she had exactly this lesson for me:

"Sky reminded me of the need for patience this evening, bless her. It hasn't stopped raining since last night and when I got to field, everyone was sopping wet and Sky (big) was shaking a bit too. So I thought I'd pop out a couple of bales of hay for them to nibble in and help them warm up from the inside out. Sky in her rush to gobble up the hay (they also have about 5 acres of grazing!!) managed to get some stuck in her throat and starting having a bout of 'choke', which to those who haven't experienced it can be very frightening.

Fortunately I have had this happen a few times in the years our herd has been together so I know that it usually clears quite quickly (usually involving lots of snot and mess...) and isn't normally an emergency. It can be and can involve vets etc but normally a bit of calming and neck massaging will enable the blockage to move and all goes back to normal.

So I thought that's fine I'll just give Sky a gentle massage and help the hay 'go down'...Sky, bless her though, wasn't ready for my help and was a little stressed by the situation so asked me to leave her alone by walking away. At first, I walked after her thinking "I know best, let me help you" and she continued to walk away, gagging and clearly quite uncomfortable.

It took me a few minutes to realise that I was making it worse by 'chasing her' when she hadn't asked for my help...doh!! Then....the penny dropped and I stepped back, apologised and explained that I would be over by the water butts if she felt that she would like some help but if she was fine sorting it herself, that was ok with me and I was sorry for 'thinking I knew best'... Well a moment or two later, after I had taken the pressure off of her, she walked very deliberately over to me and basically placed her head and neck in my hands, at which point I gently massaged the blockage (that I could feel) downwards. A couple of moments, a few big gulps and big sigh later and it was all over and she wandered off to have some more hay, a little slower though this time, giving me a little snuffle as she went.

Often we are so intent on helping, we forget that our horses may not be 'ready for' or 'wanting' our help at that point and by doing so, we are actually making things worse. Thank you Sky for the reminder and for being a very special young lady xx"

"Have patience with all things but first of all with yourself" (Saint Francis de Sales)

Her transition and the lessons she has taught have been so profound that on the 24th January 2015, two and half years after she chose us, I wrote this.....

"It was a beautiful day today, cold and sunny and that meant we were able to remove Sky's rug and allow her to soak up the sun. Bless her, I hate her having to have one on but after the rainscald of last year, we can't take any chances this year.

Interestingly I think we have finally found the right combination of environment, feed, vitamins and minerals for her at long last.

Sky has taught me so much in the two and half years she's been with us and although at times, I've felt quite desperate watching her body as it has changed and adapted, not always easily, the experience has been life-changing for both of us.

Most people think I'm daft when I say this but I do believe that her body has undergone a complete transformation and detoxing of sorts and it's taken a long time to re-discover the beautiful, glowing horse that she is. It's hard to explain. Her whole stance has changed from one which always looked a bit uncomfortable and very front-loaded to one which is balanced and free.

When she first moved into our family, her joints clicked every step she took and for a young lady it always made me cringe and worry about her long term joint health. She doesn't click anymore - I'm not exactly sure when she stopped but it was a while ago now and it's so satisfying watching her walk or trot across the field without clicking and in much more fluid way.

I have heard of other horses going through the same process but to actually witness it within our own herd has been a steep, sometimes vertical, learning curve that has added to our knowledge and understanding in an immeasurable way. In hindsight, I may have done things differently but would I have learnt as much as I did? Who knows. All I know is that this beautiful young lady has an incredible spirit, one which shines

out and touches everyone who meets her. I am so very grateful and honoured that She chose us and that She has found her peace within our family and especially with her guardian and protector Gizmo. Thank you Sky-bo's"

If we allow time and space for healing in whatever form that might take (and often that may not be what we imagined or might have originally chosen), both for our horses, those around us and ourselves we can experience the gift that true growth and release can bring. If we force it, we may never be truly healed. Sometimes that can mean finding yourself in dark places, frightening places and heart-breaking places – it's not just a straight road to 'better', 'fixed' or 'well' – and sometimes things don't even need 'fixing' at all, simply understanding and accepting without judgement. Then we may have the privilege of sharing such moments as this.....

25th February 2015......

"There is one particular moment I want to share with you from the last couple of days and it is something that those who

have been following us for a while will probably understand the importance of.

As the herd now have access to the whole 12 acres, it is such a relief to know they are not standing around in the small area of mud that has formed from feeding their hay etc. Sometimes it just takes a while to understand the land you have and how to work with it better - it's always a learning process for us.

Anyway, when we arrived the other day, the whole herd were right at the other end, some grazing, some resting, some playing and it took them a while to notice we had arrived (which I love as it means they aren't waiting around all day for us, they are content and occupied with their own 'affairs'). Well, once they did, the whole herd set off into a joyful canter towards us, across the field, kicking up their heels (and clods of mud!), pushing and bumping each other playfully and 'stopping and dropping' for a roll at a particular spot about halfway to us.

But....what made my heart swell and caught my breathe was watching Sky, our TB mare carrying herself across the field in the most beautiful, balanced and wonderful canter, using her body effectively and carrying herself as if she was flying, light as a feather. I have watched her change physically in her body and been in awe of how she has learnt to 'feel' herself again and balance herself again, simply from being in a herd with space and time. She is a genuine example of how by simply being allowed to be a horse, with a stable and supportive herd family she has become the 'butterfly' I saw in her eyes over two years ago.

I certainly know there are times when we need to give a little help to our equine family but one of the most important lessons I have learnt over the last few years is that sometimes....just sometimes, what we really need to do is 'get out of the way' and let our horses and ponies heal themselves with the help of nature and by doing our best to provide an environment that facilitates their own healing......"

Heart Connections

As winter rolls around each year, there is a tendency to see it negatively; after all it usually means shorter days and more wet and cold. However, something I have leart over the last few years especially, is that winter actually just provides us with a different environment in which to communicate and build our relationships with our horses. Winter provides us with the opportunity to practice using different senses and to 'feel' as opposed to 'see' which allows us to connect on a completely different level and to be more aware of the natural world around us, how we are interacting with it and what the consequences of that interaction might be.

On the 19th November 2014 I talked about this difference.....

"I am still getting used to the dark nights when I get up to see the herd. It always takes me a few weeks to adjust to doing things by 'feel' rather than sight, however, I don't know about anyone else but I find this time of year reminds me to use my other senses and not just rely on what I can see.

I actually really enjoy it....listening to the sounds of the creatures at the field settling for the night or waking up to begin their adventures, hearing the soft wickers of the herd as they let me know where they are - each one with their own voice.

As I cannot do a 'visual' check on everyone (I do have a head torch but prefer not to use it as the bright beam of light is uncomfortable for the horses) I have to use my other senses of touch, listening and what I guess is an 'instinctual feel' having known each member of the herd for a long time.

Often in the summer it's easy to forget to connect with touch and feel, especially if you are rushing or have 'jobs' to do as most of us do and I have come home on occasion and thought "I haven't connected with (touched) Stanley...or Whipper...or whoever..." which always make me feel a little annoyed at myself for not thinking. Yes, I will have chatted away and made sure everyone was fine, had plenty to eat and drink and was healthy etc but it is possible (not necessarily right but possible) to do all those things by sight and without actually touching everyone.

I'm not talking about forcing myself on the herd and having intense cuddles or hugs or anything like that - I just mean to offer a hand and be gifted a sniff or a kiss; to gently place a hand on a shoulder and feel the warmth of your horses body and muscles press against it in connection; to open yourself up and invite your horse to rest their head on your shoulder, that type of touching (as well as the more practical checking for lumps and bumps etc) Winter and dark nights remind me of how wonderful a gift 'to touch' is, especially as I am not a 'touchy-feely' person myself.

The dark nights also provide a reminder of how we need to trust and be trustworthy when we interact with our horses. As it has been very wet the last week or so, Sky is having to wear a rug but I am constantly changing/checking it when I'm there and allowing her time without it even it's just for half an hour. Again this all has to be done in the dark and as you know we try to do everything at liberty so this simple activity includes a huge amount of trust on both sides, especially as she would prefer to be 'naked'. We are always negotiating the arrangement - I chatter away to her, asking how she is and about her day, letting her know what I'm doing, as I move around her, standing side by side with no restraints, as I remove her rug or put one on, fiddle with the straps, check the fit and ensure it's not rubbing anywhere. Sometime we walk together while we do this and this is her saying "really Mum do I have to, I'll be fine without". I take the time to explain why (those who have followed her story will know the why) and ask if she will stand for a moment while I do the belly straps and she does - to me that's huge and a massive gesture of her trust in me to always see her as who she is and treat her with the respect she deserves.

The dark nights and winter remind me of the honour it is to share my life with such beautiful open and giving souls as our herd because I need to connect on a different level, a more intuitive level.

There is something about the deep darkness of a winter evening, the chill of the breeze and awareness of being surrounded by life that reminds me of the magic that exists everywhere if only we remember to 'see' with our hearts not just our eyes"

Build It & They Will Come

Over the years I have watched as the herd welcomed people into their world and helped them heal, physically, emotionally even spiritually. I have watched as they taught young people how to be around them and how to interact with both the herd and each other. It is no surprise to me that there are a growing number of 'therapy type' programmes involving horses and other animals – the benefits for the participants are many and easy to see!

However, although I have looked into this field of work for our herd and animals, I always held back from actually starting anything due to the potential impact it may have on the generosity and kindness of the herd, let alone their mental, physical and psychological wellbeing. You see, it is an entirely different thing for a herd to choose to spend time with strangers as opposed to doing it because it has been set up that way for what is ultimately human gain. I'm not saying it's wrong, just that we need to be very careful and aware of HOW we do it, otherwise for me, at the very least we lose the naturalness and honesty of the connection. I also feel that by having a human interpreting what is happening, as programmes such as this have to do, takes away the pureness of whatever connection the horse and human may be sharing and it may be something uniquely special to them alone and not something that can be understood or interpreted or even recognized by anyone else. I hope that makes sense?

So, although I have witnessed and indeed felt myself, the power and incredible healing and grounding of the herd, I have always struggled with how that should be 'packaged' for want of a better description, to enable others to share it too. Interestingly it was exactly what was in front of me all along as this post on our blog explains......

"Ever since I watched the film 'Field of Dreams' many years ago, the line "build it and he will come" has stuck in my mind, except for me it's always been "Build and THEY will come" which I think is the classic way the line is misquoted! Somehow though, for me, that was always how it stuck in my mind and often when I'm at the field with the herd or snuggled with dogs on the sofa, the words will pop into my head and hover there for a bit like a little reminder of something I don't know I've forgotten, before fading into the magical places of my unconscious.

Over the last ten years or so, I have been working hard to create and promote The Free Spirit Ponies Project, trying more ways than I can remember to 'get the word out there' and enable people and horses to live together in a kinder, gentler way. For most of that time, I have had limited success and all of the good ideas I had seemed to stumble slightly and never quite make it to the impressive impact I'd originally envisioned for them. Every time it happens, I get a little disappointed and frustrated as we all would trying to help something we love and care deeply about grow and flourish.

The really crazy thing is, I think I've discovered the problem and the irony is the real solution was there all the time,

working away quietly as it was meant to, right under my nose! You see, for many years I kept seeing or imagining The Free Spirit Ponies Project as a 'thing', someTHING that existed and that I could 'package up' and effectively 'sell' to those I was trying to reach. I believed it was the courses and the workshops and the books and the 'giving of knowledge' and all those other things I've tried to put out there into the world and in some ways, yes, those THINGS are all part of it, of course they are but I was missing the 'bigger picture', the essence or heart of what The Free Spirit Ponies Project really is! The stupid thing is it's exactly what I wrote about perhaps a decade ago.

What I have been doing is trying to 'sell' the interactive accessories without giving people the main product for which

those accessories were meant, the amazing salad dressing without the salad....the beautiful wrapping paper without the gift........

The words "Build it and they will come" and the ever increasing number of 'images' that have been appearing in my mind supposedly randomly weren't random at all. The herd 'calling' to people....friends and family.... and communicating with people so that they asked to visit were not random events. The peace and joy on the faces of those who meet and interact with the herd, those who simply 'be' with whoever chooses to share space with them or share touch, healing or dreams with them, with no agenda, no 'programme', 'course content' or 'workshop outline' . These are not random little moments of pleasure. THIS is what The Free Spirit Ponies Project is! It is a PLACE not a THING. It is where the herd are, connected with nature and the energy of that connectedness. It is the magic that is created in that space where the herd welcome someone into their embrace and all else disappears. It is connected souls meeting, breathing, healing each other if needed and loving each other for simply being who they are.

It is a space of sanctuary for all, people and animals alike, without agenda. A place where peace and awareness can grow without restriction, where connection with nature can be re-established and all beings can find themselves and become whole again. One of our herd, now in spirit, talked about 'soul retrieval' in a communication we had not so long ago and I finally think I understand what she was referring to because I have now seen it and felt it, not just for myself but for members of the herd and for some of the people who have visited. That is not an 'accessory' I can package up and take to people, they need to experience it and feel it with every fibre of their being.

For all this time, I have been looking in the 'wrong place' quite literally for the answers I needed and all the time, they were there quietly happening despite my distraction and frustration. The most humbling part of this realisation though is that it has nothing to do with me and everything to do with the herd. I have been misinterpreting my 'role' as taking the message out there, trying to 'bottle up and distribute' what they wanted to

137

say and while that is still part of the 'accessory package' the truth is in fact that all I really needed to do was create a space in which the magic could happen, send out the invitations and step back and let it be – well...and maybe provide the odd cuppa!

I now know what (at least in a feeling sense) The Free Spirit Ponies Project is. It is a place where all are welcome to spend time; sitting beneath the trees, listening to the breeze whispering through the branches; standing with one of the herd, breathing together and connecting; sitting reading a book in the shade with bare feet on the grass; enveloped in the smells of the herb garden or lost in the sounds of willow branches swaying and birds singing. It is a place where souls can reconnect with the wisdom and heartbeat of the earth, a place to be without fear or judgement and without agenda, learning to hear their own heart and the voice of earth around them. It is a space for people to think, write, listen, sing, dance or simply be still and rejuvenate....whatever they need and it is a space for nature, the herd and any other animals who find their way to our family to live, grow, thrive and be who they

truly are and it is a space for us to share with each other. It is a small sanctuary in what can be a sometimes crazy, often frustrating, occasionally heart-breaking world and it is a glimpse of what can be and what could be......and what is, if only we stopped for a moment and opened our hearts"

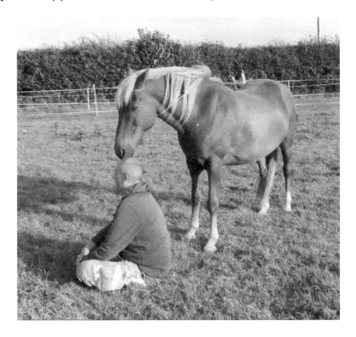

The piece of writing I talked about in this chapter is the presented to you over the next few pages. As you read, try to imagine what it would be like, feel like, sound like.........

Are you ready to come with me to Free Spirit Farm?

Finding Free Spirit

I wrote this possibly a decade ago when someone asked me what my dream was. I went away after trying to explain it and a while later, sat down and put it into words.

My original handwritten manuscript revealed itself while I was looking for something a while ago, just at a time when I was having one of those "what am I doing?" blips and suddenly I remembered.

This is my dream, this is what The Free Spirit Ponies is - at the moment it's a place in my heart and in the hearts of our herd and animal family but I have a feeling that sometime soon you may be able to find that little battered old sign and come and visit....This is my dream......................

FINDING FREE SPIRIT......

Free Spirit Farm is a wonderful place.

It's tucked away down a quiet country lane, set back slightly from the road.

You almost wouldn't know it's there except for the tiny weathered sign hanging, just in the right place; it's metal chain chinking slightly whenever there's a breeze. It hangs from the aged branch of a huge friendly looking oak tree that almost seems to guide you into the small gravel driveway with its strong welcoming branches.

More trees line the short drive to the equally weathered wooden gates which guard the entrance to this little paradise.

On the gate is, what was once, a brightly coloured nameplate, now faded and worn by the years, but somehow warmer and more inviting because of this. It reads "Welcome to Free Spirit Farm – welcome home".

The gravel driveway extends around to the right to an area where you park your car, sheltered by a ramshackle copse of trees and bushes. There are no individual bays or lines or even any signs telling you what to do or where to park but you won't even notice that until you leave and realise it couldn't be any other way.

The entrance gates themselves are tall and solid and very, very old. They look like they would take a great effort to open them but they glide open with a single touch of a tentative fingertip, without a single creak or groan, hinting at the love and compassion that will be found inside.

I would defy even the most hardened and bitter of human being to be unmoved by the scene that fills your senses in that first glimpse of the farm. It is from this moment that you start to see and feel the magic.

Instantly you are overcome with the natural beauty of this tiny haven and you become aware that you seem to have left your worries and stresses behind in the car park, although you won't remember doing it.

The strong solid wooden gates close quietly and gracefully behind you and a new world opens up before your eyes.

Just as you think you might just be frozen in the moment, a small black and white cat purrs at your feet and winds itself around and between your legs, begging for a cuddle. This is Patch, the un-official welcoming party, who like everyone and everything else on the farm, does what comes naturally to him. Nobody told him or trained him to do it......he just does.
Once he's said hello, Patch starts to walk towards what seems to be the centre of the farm, urging you to follow with a gently encouraging meow.

On your left is a small thatched cottage, with very well established roses climbing higgledy-piggledy across the front walls. A small wisp of smoke winds slowly out of the chimney and the smell of fresh baked bread fills your nose as you walk past.

The garden which wraps itself around the cottage as if embracing it, is not tidy or ordered – if anything, it is completely the opposite, with far more natural flowers, trees and bushes than any that have been consciously planted there over the years.

There is no pattern or order to the garden except the one that Mother Nature intended. What might have once been a lawn has been decorated in numerous places with splashes of colour from more flowers and bulbs than its possible to count, poking through the rich deep green of the grass, their heads lifted up to smile at the warming sun.

Tucked away under the trailing branches of an enormous willow are two hives, worn so the edges are softened and rounded by years of use and weather; the soft humming of the bees that live there travels gently on the breeze to reach your ears.

Sparrows and starlings flit between the branches of the dark green bushes, carrying food back to their young, tucked away in one of the many hidden and well used nests.

Although the garden is clearly well loved and cared for, it is apparent that it is Mother Nature who decides what flourishes here. It is also obvious that she has a knowledgeable eye because the garden is beautiful and inviting and smells intoxicating.

Just beyond the cottage is another small gate which leads to an orchard and beyond that a large meadow. On the left of the meadow is a huge barn, weathered and ramshackle like everything else. Everything about its presence, partly tucked away into the woodlands behind, makes you realise it's been here a long time and will be here for a long time to come.

Up until this point it is possible to have not noticed the sounds of the farm, there is so much beauty for the eyes to see and such a peaceful harmonious atmosphere, that you could be mistaken for thinking that it is silent. The truth is that Free Spirit Farm is in fact a very noisy place – it's just that the sounds are all those of nature living and breathing in harmony. These sounds complement each other and are calming and soothing to the human ear - it's just that we, in our busy lives, have forgotten to listen for them.

Along one side of the orchard is a gurgling spring, spurting water from deep in the earth and bubbling down into a small, perfectly formed, stream that runs all of the way around the meadow beyond.

As your eyes follow the journey of the babbling brook, you will start to see the other inhabitants of this little haven. Head bent low, taking a long slow drink from the stream is a sandy coloured pony. Alongside him, a small black and white pig, splashing her nose in the water and rolling around the muddy bank.

As you scan around the meadow and the orchard, suddenly the wonder of the farm becomes clear.

Under the boughs of one of the many apple trees another pig, black this time, sunbathes as a small black and white goat tries to nibble the grass between her ears. Several other ponies are grazing together in the middle of the meadow and tucked between them are three sheep, enthusiastically cropping the bits of grass the ponies are choosing to leave.

There are chickens, ducks and geese everywhere – all colours, shapes and sizes, pecking at the grass; dust-bathing under the trees or simply strutting between the legs of the other animals and you are likely to wonder how you didn't see them before.

Take a walk over to the barn and you will sense the soul of this place; the heart that beats bringing it all together.

There are no pens, no stables, no enclosures or designated areas. The barn is completely open inside and the smell of the fresh, soft straw that carpets the floor is unmistakable and surprisingly welcoming.

Look closer and you will see a small Shetland pony, lying in a corner sleeping peacefully and dreaming deeply. Snuggled between his legs is a pink pig, her head buried in the straw, snoring happily. If you look really closely, you may even see a little foot twitching or an ear flicking as they dream of apples and playing in the sun.

In another corner, several chickens are sitting or choosing where to lay their eggs.

Over to the right, a sheep is feeding her two lambs, while others play in the straw, trying to convince a nearby goat to join in.

Take a step back and allow yourself to see the farm as a whole, living and breathing in harmony and you will become aware that this is a place like no other. Yet it feels absolutely as if this is exactly as it should be; how it's supposed to be – animals, nature and people living as one.

There are no rules and regulations, no bars or cages, no demands or duties, just life at its purest, brightest and most surprising. As you stand and watch, embraced by the safety and comfort of the atmosphere, having completely forgotten the stresses and rigidness of the outside world, you will have a sense of coming home.

I still do every day but I am lucky....because this is my home and I share it with the animals, plants, insects and birds. I experience every day the deep joy of letting go and allowing nature to decide and of being part of her amazing creations.

The front gate is always unlocked.

If you happen to be driving down a quiet country lane this way and you notice a small, weathered sign, hanging from the branch of an old oak tree.....pull in and come and share it with me.

Everyone is welcome.

ONE FINAL MESSAGE….well for now anyway!

Adapted from an entry I made on our Facebook page on 23rd December 2014….

Remember to reflect on what's happened, what you've achieved, how far you have come and perhaps what you are planning for the future.

Life has its share of heartbreak such as when we lose those closest to us be they human or animal who, although are no longer here with us physically, are always with us in our hearts.

It has also had its share of laughter and joy – for me recently this has included the puppies Indiana and Shilo arriving, writing my first book, watching Sky flourish at last and the herd living every moment in the way only they can.

In reality I guess most years when we look back tend to balance themselves out, even if sometimes it doesn't feel like it until we look back and reflect with gratitude.

For me this journey has been particularly special. I have grown in my understanding and awareness more in the last few years than ever before and I have the horses and ponies, who through their patience and compassion have guided me, to thank for the peace and contentment I now feel, both with myself, with the life I have and where this journey is leading.

The herd and the horses and ponies who have been part of my life have gifted me so many unique lessons, some that at the time I didn't understand and some that caused me to react negatively but I have learned that that's ok…in fact it is important to honour and accept both the good and the not so good in ourselves – it is what makes us whole and in doing so we can learn from every experience not just the ones we choose to.

I have been reminded of the gift of joy and movement and exhilaration and then of being still and quiet and 'in the moment'. I have (and still am) being taught how to 'let go' and 'accept without trying to control' but also how to 'stand up and be counted' when called upon to do so and to be true to myself, even when I am most vulnerable.

I have been shown and taught even more than I thought I knew already, about the fact that the horses around us are truly compassionate and spiritual beings that have the power to heal and teach and love in a way most of us can only dream of. There are so many more 'lessons'.

One of my favourite quotes is "*When we go to them and they walk away we should pause.....and consider....They may be saying "Where you are, in this moment, is not the right place. Follow me to a place closer to my world. It is there where I will show you how to heal*" (Healing Horses 2013) – I have learnt to follow the lead of our horses rather than the other way around and the 'places' they are showing me are breath-taking.

There is a legend which tells how because of the magic that exists, animals can speak to us on Christmas Eve – the truth is that magic is there every day and they can speak to us whenever they choose to and in fact are, all the time..... In the words of Kate Solisti-Mattelon "*Horses are persistently hopeful that humanity will wake up*".....it's time we finally listen to what they have to say.

About the Author

I have loved horses all of my life but was only able to realize the dream of learning to ride at the age of 21 when I was working in a job that paid me a good enough salary. I still vividly remember those first lessons, learning how to rise in trot, surrounded by a group of 10 and 11 year olds who were happily cantering as if they'd been born on horseback!

I dreamt of owning a horse of my own but never thought it really possible. Then, around 2001, some devastating personal events proved to be a major turning point for me and before long I was working with horses every day and had bought my first pony, Stanley, a Connemara cross, who I still have and who has been my 'rock' and partner through many a down time.

Circumstances changed again and after much soul searching and logical, rational and calculated decision making (not easy for an emotional person like myself), I became the owner of six more wonderful ponies including a miniature Shetland, three New Forest ponies and two Welsh ponies.

Suddenly my dream had come true in more ways than I could ever have imagined possible. However, that, I quickly realised, was only the start of the journey and over the last twelve years I have been constantly learning what it takes to become a true horsewoman in the eyes of my horses.

The journey has pitted me against many of the long-upheld and traditional practices of horse-keeping and there have been times when I almost gave in and just did what everyone else did but my horses prevented me from doing that and I will be eternally grateful to them.

We are now up to ten in the herd and have been able to include mares, including a 16.3hh TB – fortune worked her magic and found us a bigger field which meant we could offer a lifetime home to more horses/ponies and also create an environment that encouraged health and happiness.

Our horses and ponies live as a herd, outdoors, 24/7 without rugs (except in extreme circumstances) or shoes and are allowed to express their personalities and natural instincts in whichever way they choose. They share their field with two miniature pigs called Norman and Percy and an abundance of wildlife and continually challenge me to be true to myself and what I've learnt.

My goal is to share their 'magic' with others.

One of the things that used to really bother me about the horse world is that our horses and ponies are still seen as possessions or 'things' to enable us to take part in certain activities. For example, I am always being asked "What do you do with them (i.e. my ponies)?" For years, this really annoyed me because I found myself trying to 'make up' exciting things that I 'did' with my ponies so I didn't seem 'different'. Not any more though, now my answer is something like "I enjoy their time and company as friends and occasionally, we might go for a ride together". The expressions on people's faces are usually amusing as they struggle with what I've said and responses vary from "Oh...that's nice" to "Well I think it's cruel to not do anything with your horses". Not everyone but sadly most!

It was while mulling over another of these conversations that the idea for The Free Spirit Ponies project came to me. I realised that in reality I actually do a great deal with my ponies, none of which involves getting on their backs and the more I thought about it, the more the list of 'things' I did' grew longer! Every day I think of something else or try something else, so my list will keep growing as will, hopefully, my relationship with and understanding of my horses and the other animals around me. The thing I do most though is to learn from them and spend time with them as friends.

This is a journey and I have no idea where the end will be or if there even is an ending (I hope not actually) but I plan to enjoy every step!

If you would like to follow the journey with us, have a look at and 'like' our page on Facebook – "The Free Spirit Ponies".

https://www.facebook.com/pages/The-Free-Spirit-Ponies/301243569904837

https://thefreespiritponies.wordpress.com/

L - #0072 - 180419 - C0 - 210/148/8 - PB - DID2497289